Tips

▶ Help your child focus on the tasks by minimizing distractions such as television.

▶ Explain directions before your child begins a new type of activity.

▶ Check your child's work and help correct errors. Praise a job well done!

▶ Encourage your child to talk about the work. For example, what did he or she like or not like about the task?

Supplies

▶ scissors

▶ glue stick or glue

▶ crayons or colored pencils

▶ marking pens

▶ pencil

▶ clear tape

Table of Contents

Listen for the Sound

Color the things that begin with the sound of m.

Mm

Are there 3 in a row?

yes   no

Cookies!

Count the cookies. Draw a line to the number that tells how many.

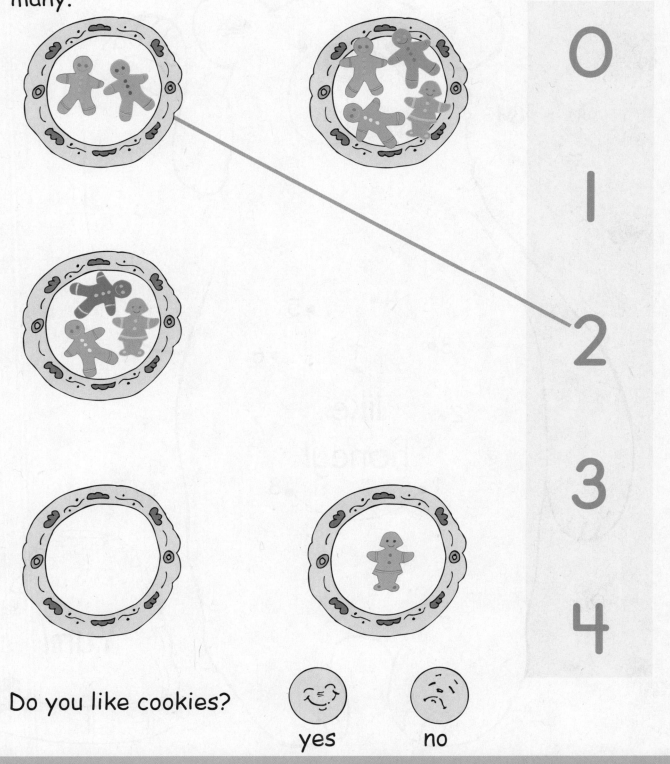

Do you like cookies?

yes   no

Bees and Bear

Connect the dots. Color the bear brown.

4•   •5

3•   •6

I

2•   like   •7

honey!

1•   •8

Yum!

Chug, Chug!

Color the shapes:

train

7

What Will I Wear?

Match them up.

8

Button, Button

Cut and paste. Sort the buttons.

Blue Buttons

Red Buttons

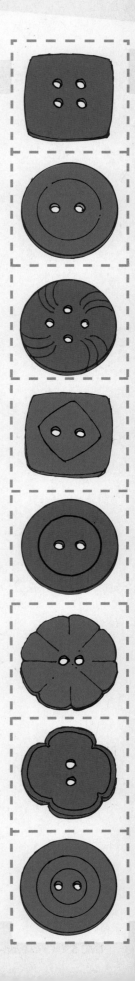

What is alike about all the blue buttons?

1 hole   2 holes   3 holes

Where Is Alf's Bone?

Help Alf find his bone.

10

Happy Octopus

Trace the numbers.

Count.

1 __ 3 __ 5 __ 7 __

My octopus has _____ arms.

What Shoes Shall I Wear?

Match.

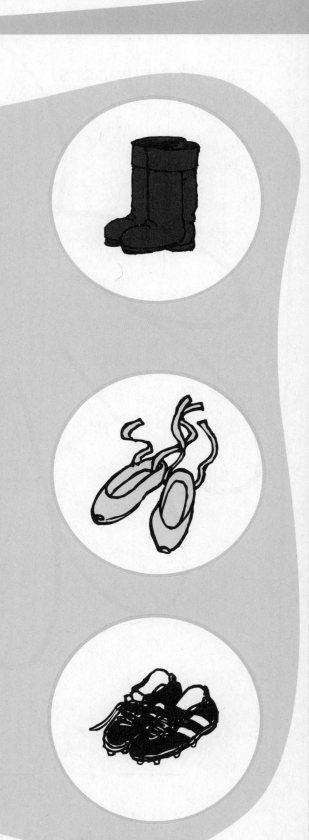

Make a Book

Cut. ✂ Staple on the side.

THAT'S ONE MORE MOUSE

One mouse
One mouse nibbling at my door.

1

$2 + 1 = \boxed{}$

Then one more...
Three mice nibbling at my door.

3

1 + 1 =

staple

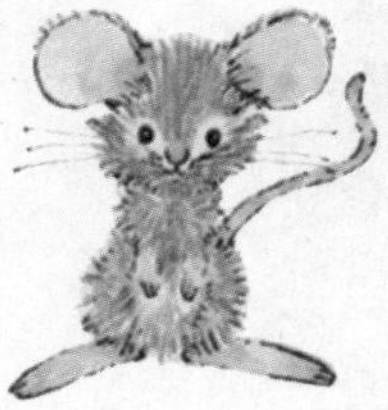

Then one more...
Two mice nibbling at my door.

2

staple

EMC 6308 • © Evan-Moor Corp.

The Never-Bored Kid Book 2

3 + 1 =

staple

Then one more...
Four mice nibbling at my door.

4

staple

EMC 6308 • © Evan-Moor Corp.

The Never-Bored Kid Book 2

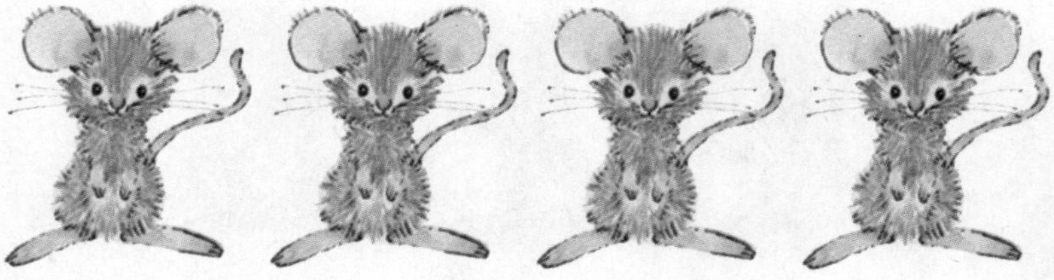

Name That Color!

Fill in the boxes.

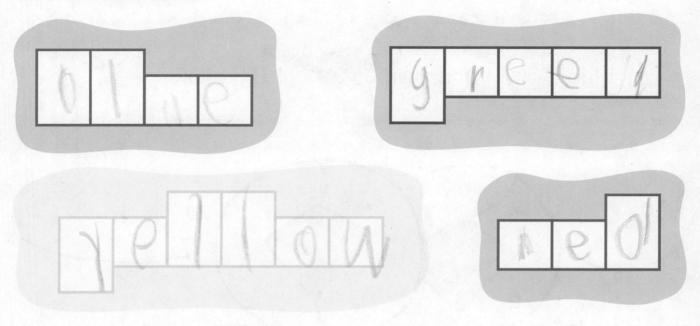

blue

green

yellow

red

WORD BOX

red   **blue**

yellow   **green**

Color.

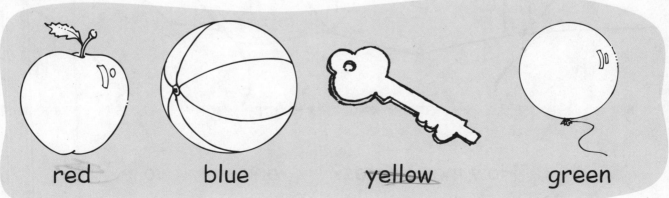

red   blue   yellow   green

Tweet Tweet

Color each part.

h=blue   **n**=brown   **u**=yellow

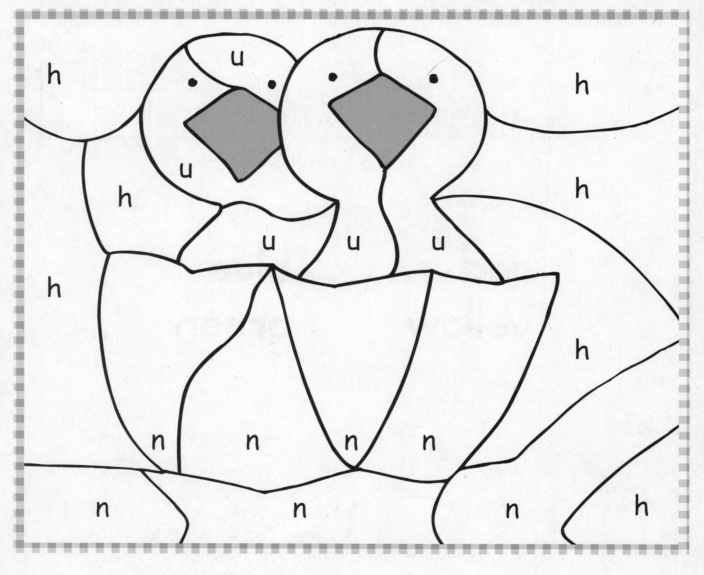

How many birds?   one   two

Up and Down

Color the picture. Trace the words.

down

up

Color the picture. Circle the correct word.

up   down

up   down

Five Red Apples

Read and count.

One for    5 − 1 = ☐

One for    4 − 1 = ☐

One for    3 − 1 = ☐

One for    2 − 1 = ☐

One red apple for me!

Fish Spots

Cut and paste the fish.
Count the dots on each fish.

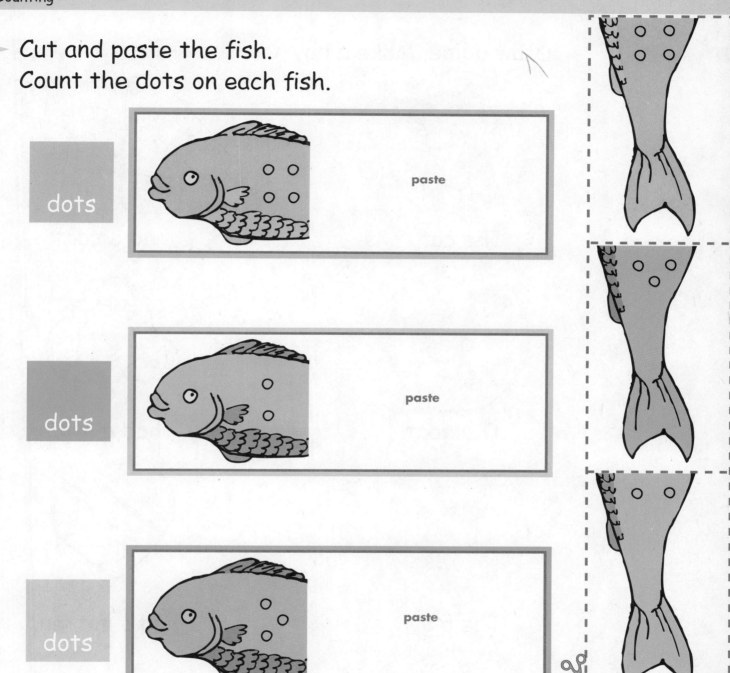

dots

paste

dots

paste

dots

paste

Which fish has the most dots?

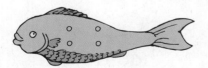 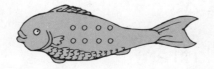 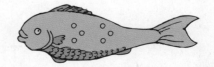

19

Getting Dressed!

Draw a line. Make a rhyme.

The cat

had a coat.

The goat

had a wig.

The pig

had a mitten.

The kitten

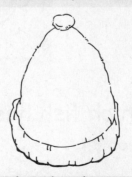

had a hat.

Listen for the Sound

Letter/Sound Association

Color the things that begin with the sound of l.

Are there 3 in a row?

 yes   no

How Would You Feel?

Circle happy or sad.

happy

sad

happy

sad

happy

sad

happy

sad

happy

sad

happy

sad

Who Is It?

Color to find the surprise.

What Will Happen?

Draw a line. Show what will happen.

24

On or Off?

Opposites

Trace on and off.

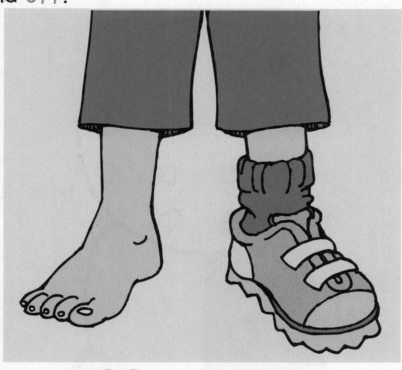

off   on

Circle.

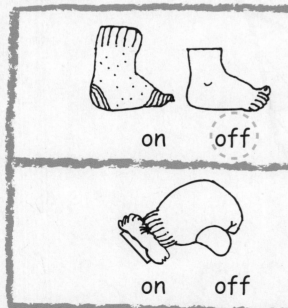

on   (off)

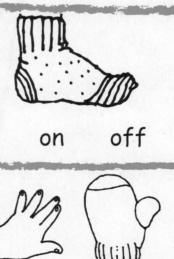

on   off

on   off

on   off

Ice Cream

Color to match.

Trace.

ice cream

Little Bo Peep

Help her find her pet.

Turtle

Connect the dots. Start with 1.

Count the turtles.

The Never-Bored Kid Book 2

Frogs, Frogs, Frogs

Cut and paste.

2 + 2 = ☐

1 + 2 = ☐

3 + 2 = ☐

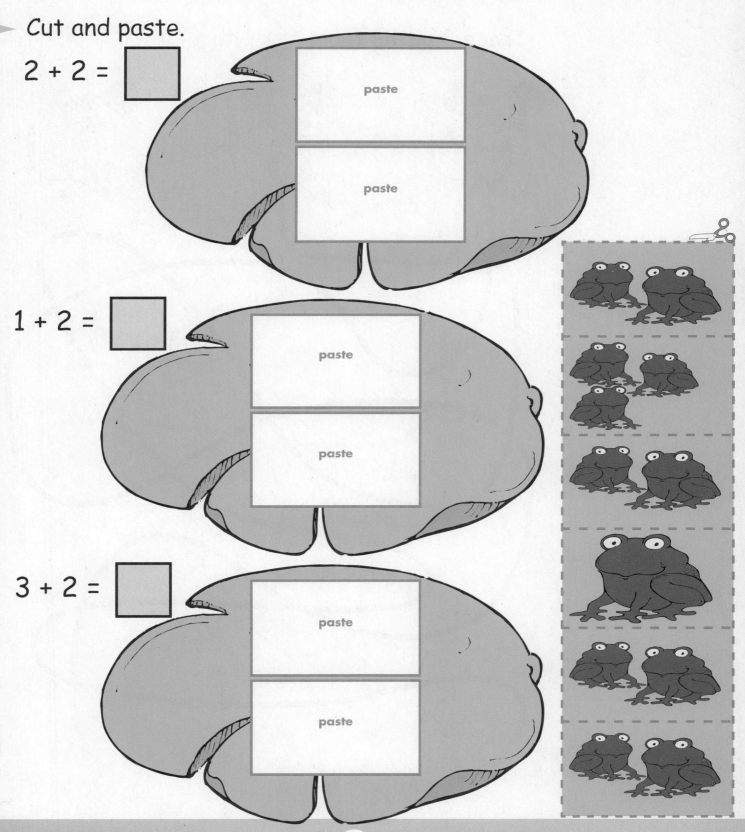

Cheese Treats

Trace 3 paths from 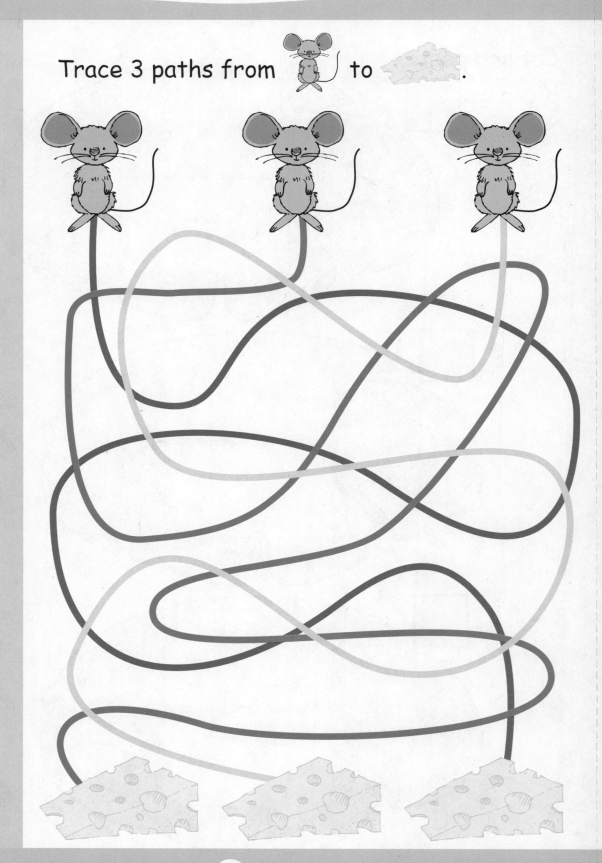 to .

30

Find Red

Trace and color.

Find red and circle.

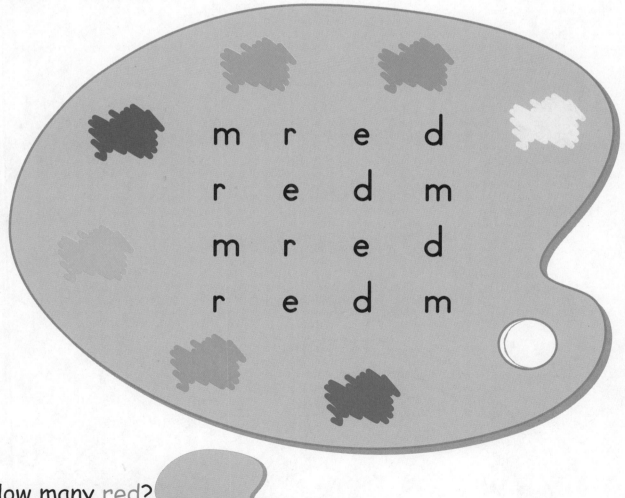

m r e d

r e d m

m r e d

r e d m

How many red? _____

Blast Off!

Draw a rocket. Count down to blast off.

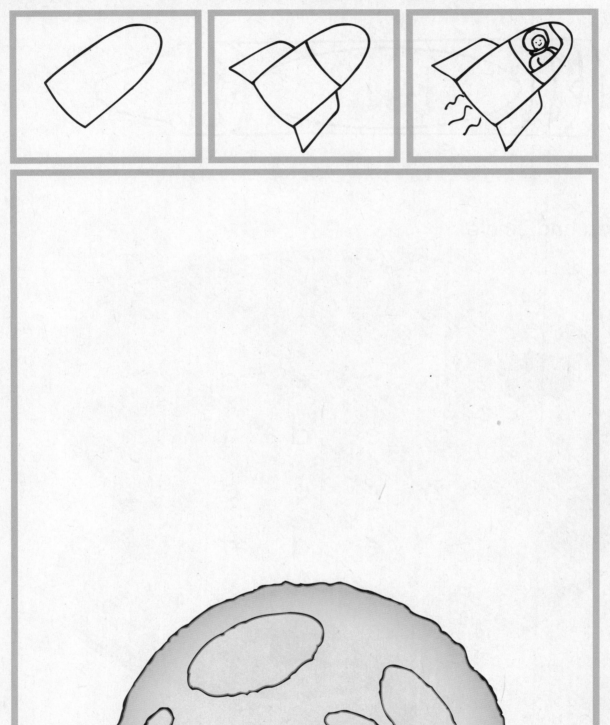

10
9
8
7
6
5
4
3
2
1

Blast off!

Listen for the Sound

Letter/Sound Association

Color the things that begin with the sound of f.

Ff

Are there 3 in a row?

yes   no

What Will It Be?

Draw a picture to show what it will be.

34

Make a Book

Color. Cut. ✂ Staple on the side.

WHERE DOES IT SLEEP?

bed

nest

cave

My book:

1

EMC 6308 • © Evan-Moor Corp.   The Never-Bored Kid Book 2

In a nest.

3

In a cave.

2

The Never-Bored Kid Book 2

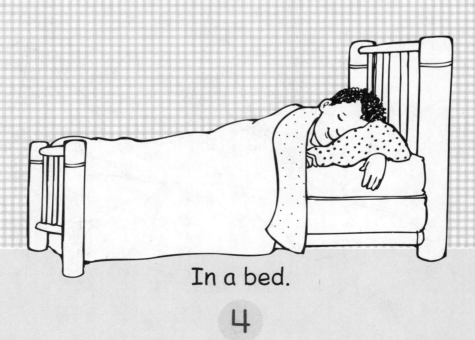

In a bed.

4

The Never-Bored Kid Book 2

36 The Never-Bored Kid Book 2

staple

staple

staple

staple

Color Fun

Write the words.

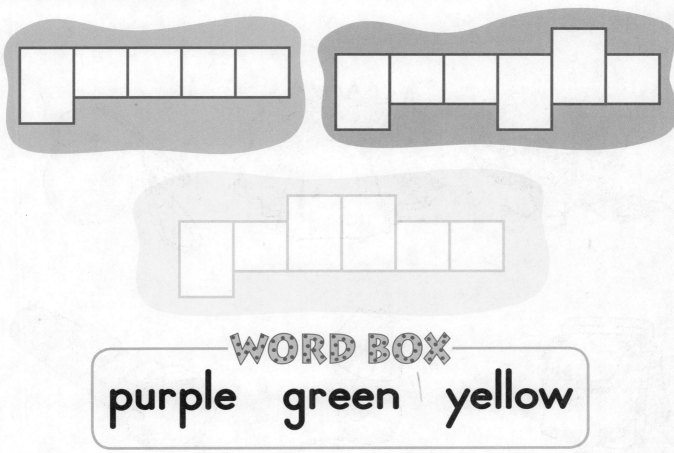

WORD BOX

purple green yellow

Color it.

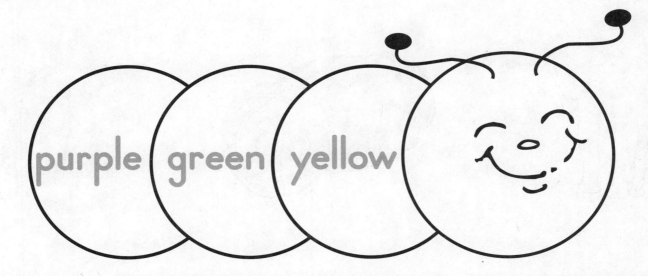

Going Camping

Circle what you would take on a camping trip.

38

9, 10, A Big Fat _____

Draw lines to connect the dots. Start with 1.

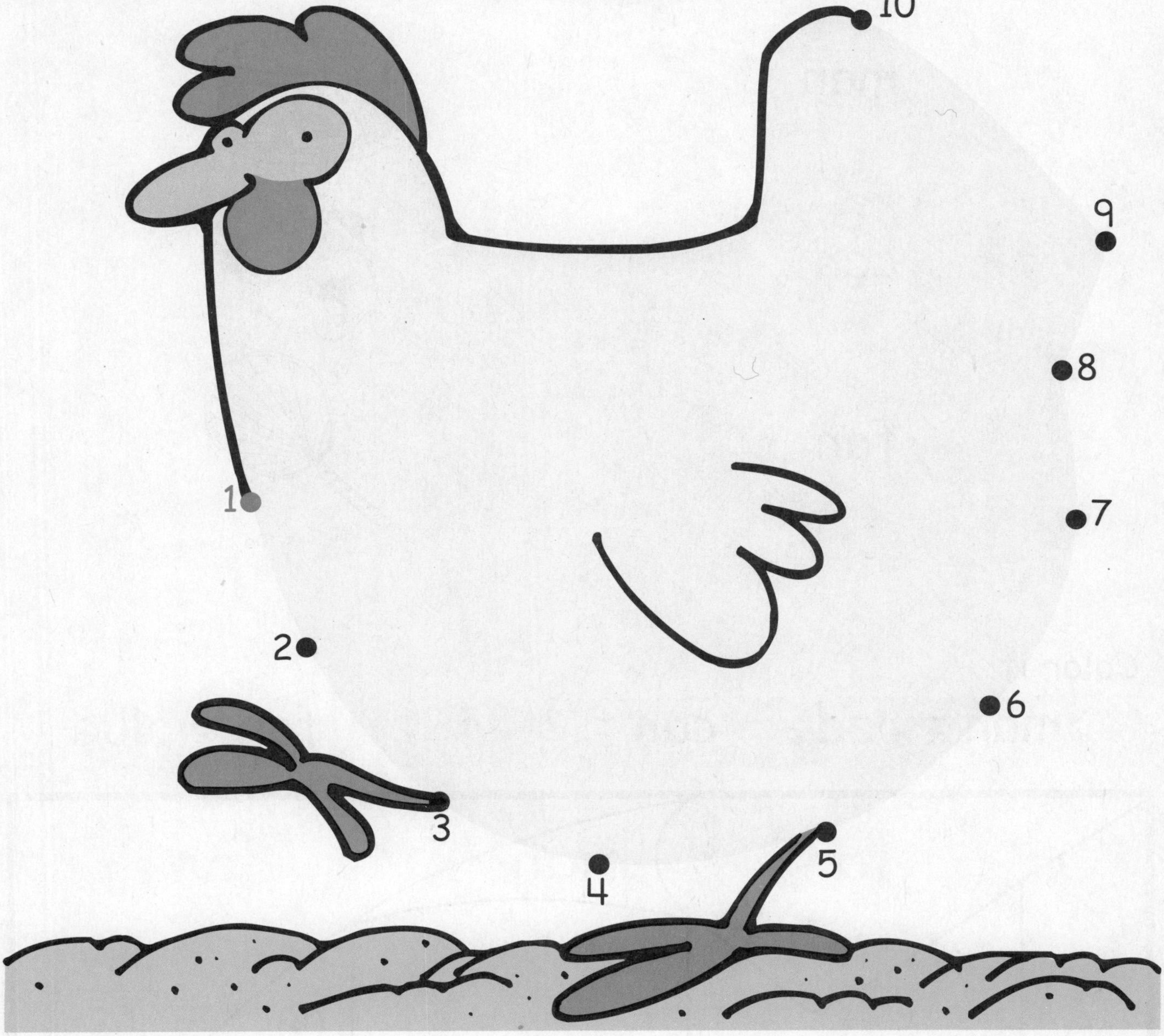

Trace.

1 2 3 4 5

6 7 8 9 10

I Can Rhyme

Draw a line from the word to the picture.

man

can

fan

Color it.

man = red   **can = yellow**   **fan = blue**

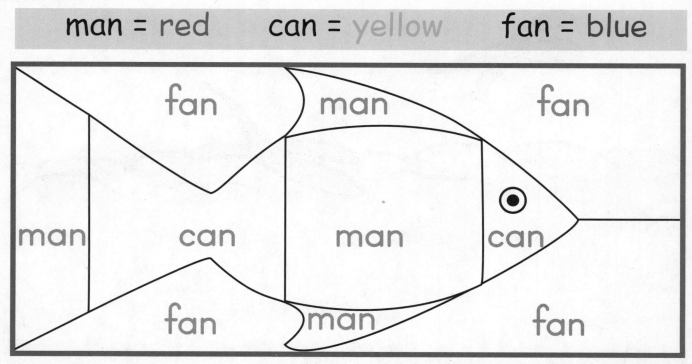

Fill It!

Cut. Paste.

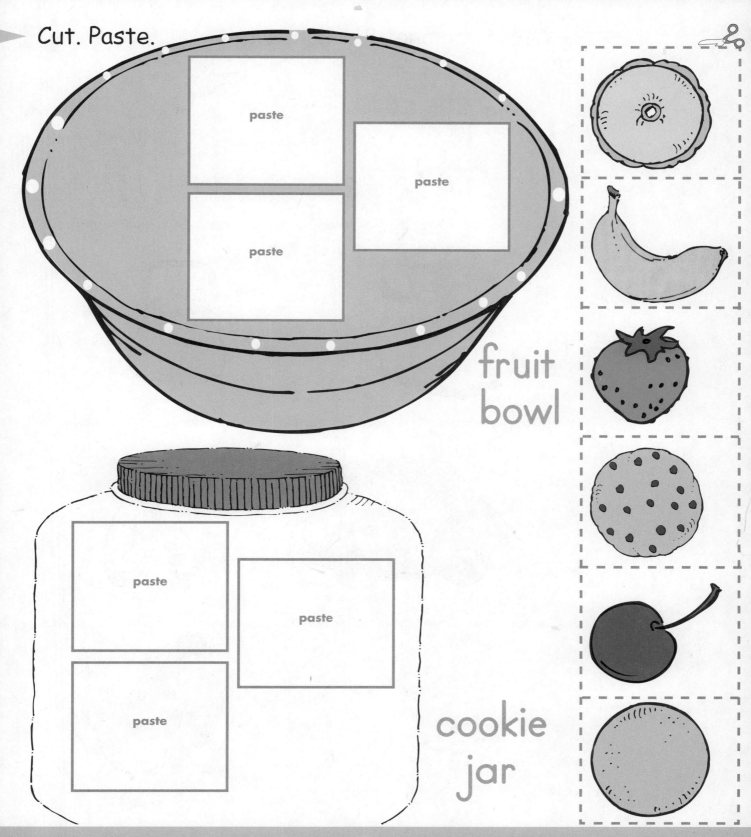

paste

paste

paste

fruit bowl

paste

paste

paste

cookie jar

Which Is Heavier?

Circle the one that is heavier.

42

Jack and Jill

Trace a path for Jack. Trace a path for Jill.

Jack and Jill
Went up the hill
To fetch a pail of water.
Jack fell down
And broke his crown
And Jill came tumbling after.

Have a Slice

Connect the dots. Start with 1.

How many seeds in this slice? _____

44

Colorful Squares!

Match the parts that make a square.

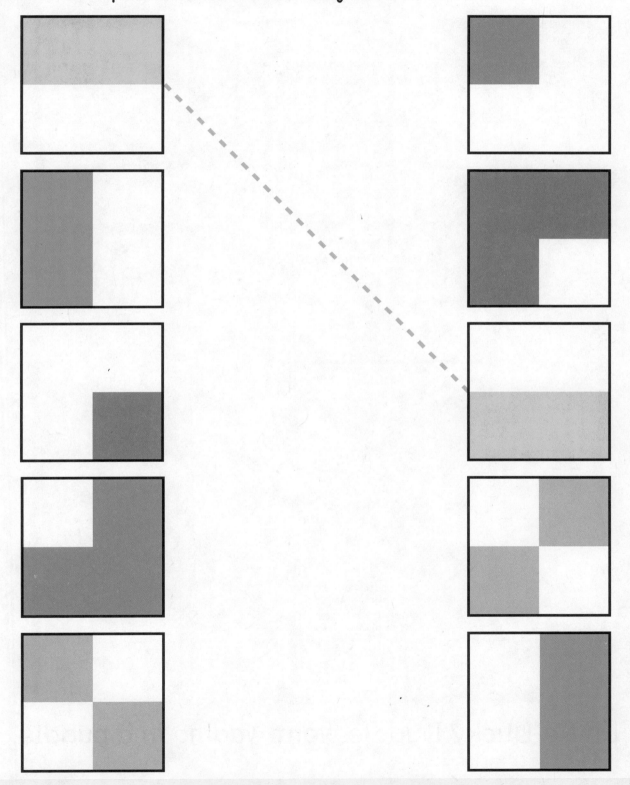

45

Little Ducky Duddle

Draw Ducky Duddle.

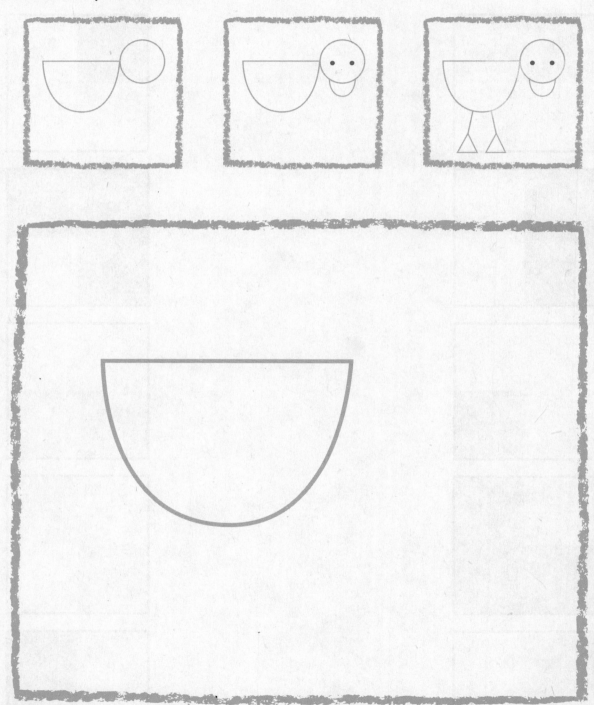

Little Ducky Duddle went wading in a puddle.

I Can Count

Trace the numbers.

10	9	8	7	6	5	4	3	2	1

Count backward from 10 to 1. Color the boxes.

Start

10	9	0	1	4
6	8	5	2	10
3	7	4	8	9
0	6	5	4	4
4	3	8	3	5
5	2	7	2	1

Finish

Piggy Bank

Connect the dots. Start with 1. Count the pennies.

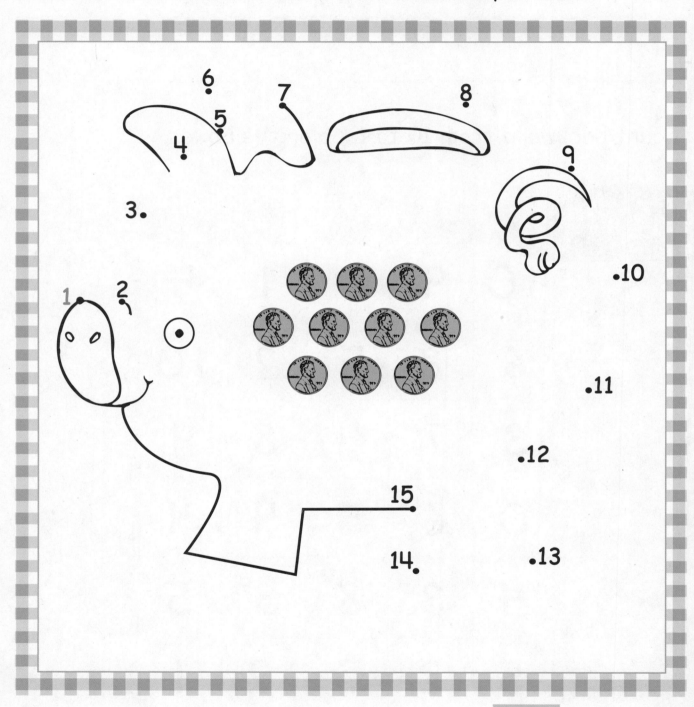

How many pennies in the bank?

The Three Little Pigs

Cut and paste the finger puppets. Use the puppets to retell the story of The Three Little Pigs.

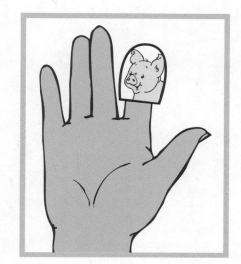

50

Listen for the Sound

Color the things that begin with the sound of **d**.

Are there 3 in a row?

 yes   no

Where Is Maddy Going?

Maddy has a .

Maddy has a ✏️ .

Maddy has a .

Maddy has a 🎒 .

Maddy is going to the _____ .

school

park

beach

Elmer Elephant

Color the shapes.

Circle what Elmer would like to eat.

Wiggle Worm

Continue the pattern.

54

Helicopter Tricks

Help the helicopter land.

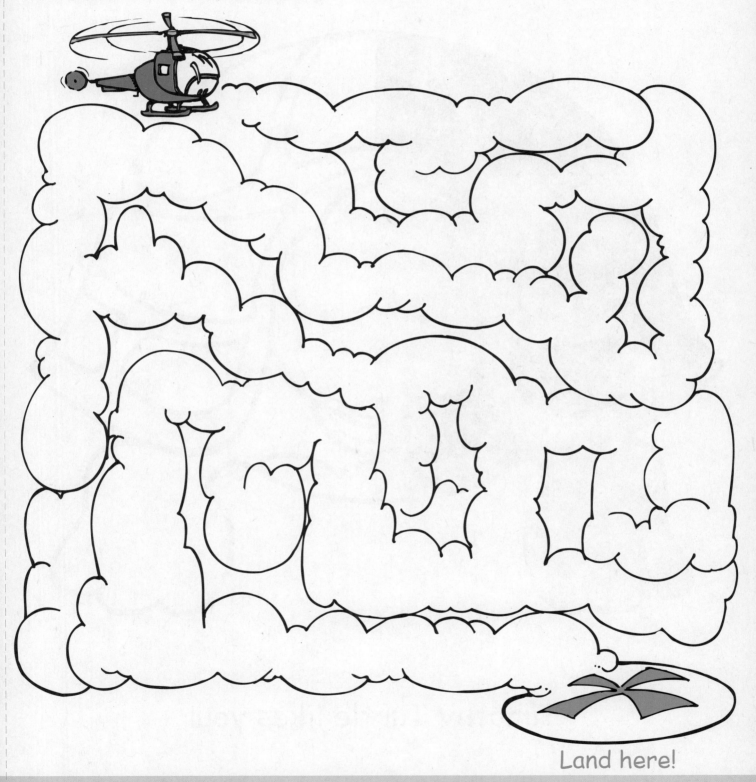

Land here!

55

Visual Discrimination

Color to match.

Timothy Turtle likes you!

Bugs Galore!

Solve the problems.

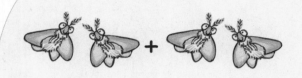

$$2 + 2 = \boxed{}$$

$$4 + 2 = \boxed{}$$

$$3 + 3 = \boxed{}$$

$$2 + 3 = \boxed{}$$

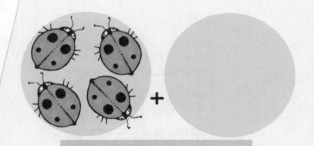

$$4 + 0 = \boxed{}$$

$$1 + 3 = \boxed{}$$

Just the Same

Match the shapes.

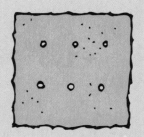

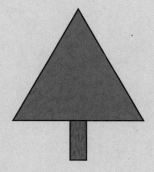

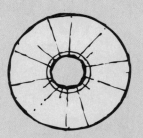

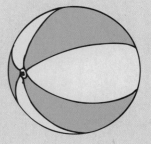

Clancy the Clown

Draw Clancy.

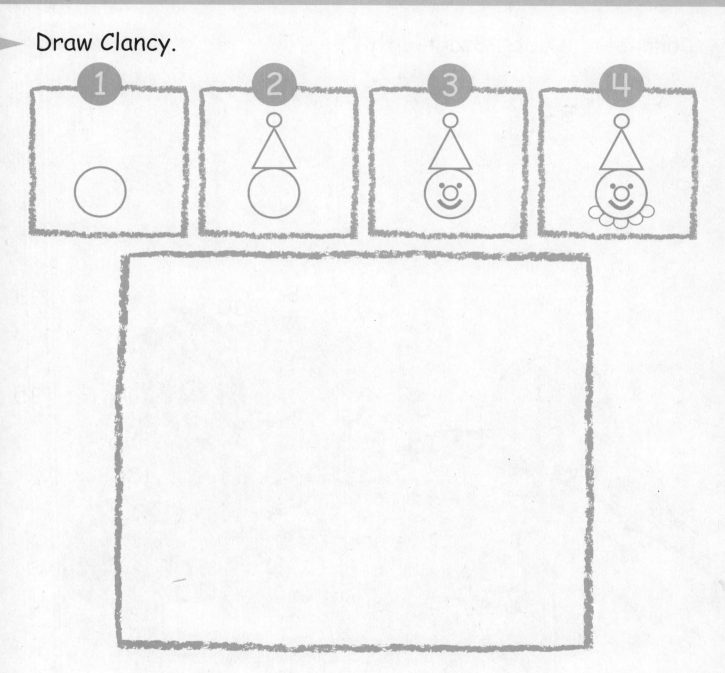

Clancy Clown is funny!

Draw a 🎈 for him.

Good Morning!

Connect the dots. Start with 1.

5 •   7 •   9 •

                                    11 •

3 •

                8 •
            6 •   10 •   13 •
        4 •
        2 •   12 •
    1 •   14 •   15 •
                                    16 •
                                18 •   17 •

Rise and shine!

Find the Rhyme

Cut and paste.

fan

| paste |

hat

| paste |

dog

| paste |

skate

| paste |

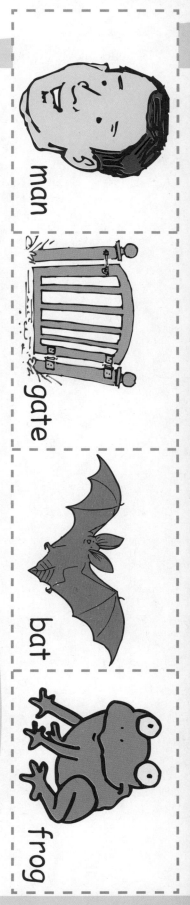

man

gate

bat

frog

Color Fun!

Color to match.

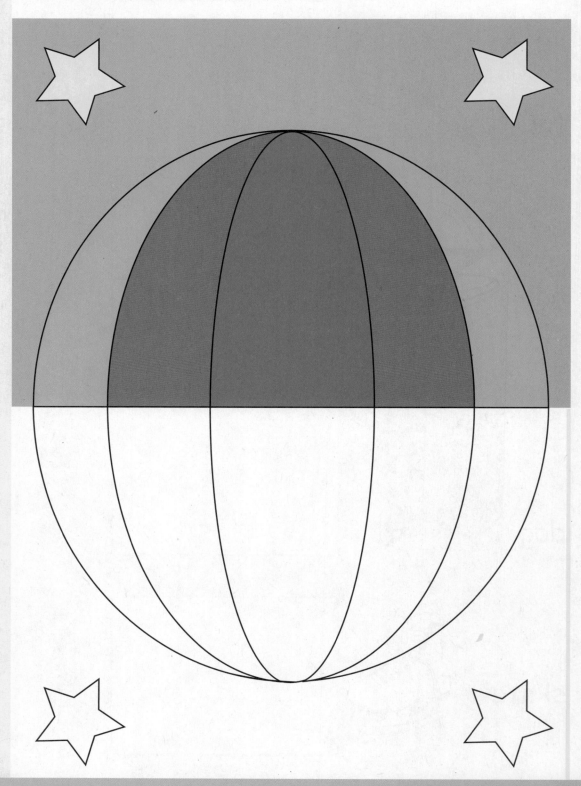

How Much?

Count what is left.

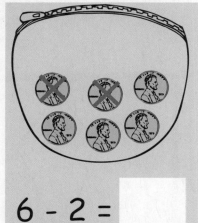

6 - 2 =

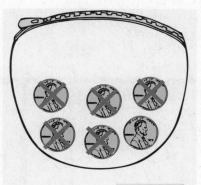

6 - 5 =

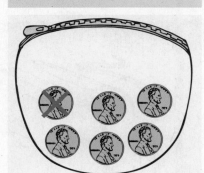

6 - 1 =

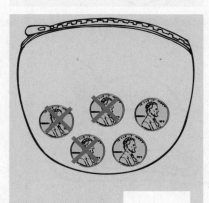

5 - 3 =

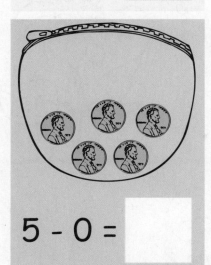

5 - 0 =

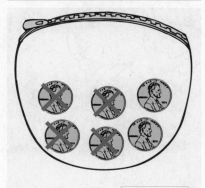

6 - 4 =

Listen for the Sound

Color the things that begin with the sound of t.

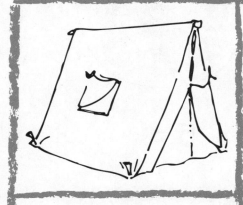  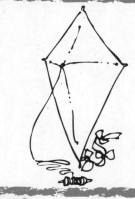

 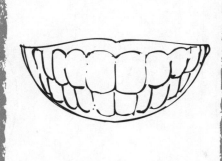 

Are there 3 in a row?

 yes   no

What's Inside?

Draw a line to show what is inside each package.

65

A Shape Picture

Color the shapes.

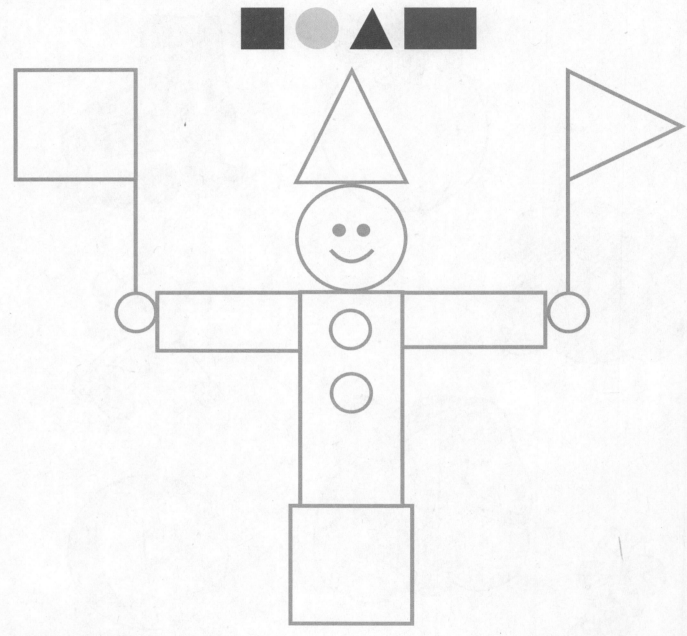

Count the shapes.

Make a Book

Cut. ✂ Staple on the side.

MISS MUFFET

Little Miss Muffet
Sat on a tuffet.

1

EMC 6308 • © Evan-Moor Corp. The Never-Bored Kid Book 2

Along came a spider
That sat down beside her

3

EMC 6308 • © Evan-Moor Corp. The Never-Bored Kid Book 2

Eating her curds and whey.

2

EMC 6308 • © Evan-Moor Corp.   The Never-Bored Kid Book 2

And frightened Miss Muffet away.

EMC 6308 • © Evan-Moor Corp.   The Never-Bored Kid Book 2

Put It in Order

Color, cut, and paste.

1

paste

2

paste

3

paste

4

paste

Robots Big and Little

Count the blocks.

blocks tall

blocks tall

blocks tall

Rock-a-Bye Baby

Color what Baby needs.

71

Flying High

Color to match.

I
see

kites.

Where Will You See Me?

Cut and paste.
Put the vehicles in the correct place.

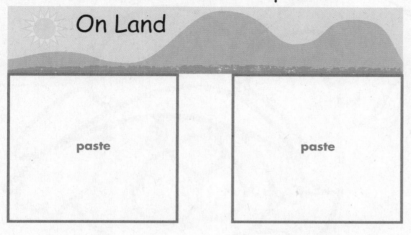

On Land

paste	paste

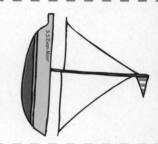

In the Air

paste	paste

At Sea

paste	paste

Let's Take a Ride

red
yellow
green
black

yellow
red
green
yellow
green
red
green
black
black

Count the Scoops

Color the ice cream. Tell how many scoops.

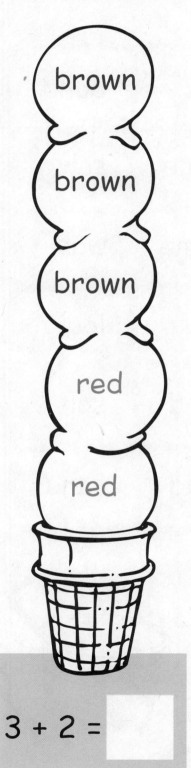
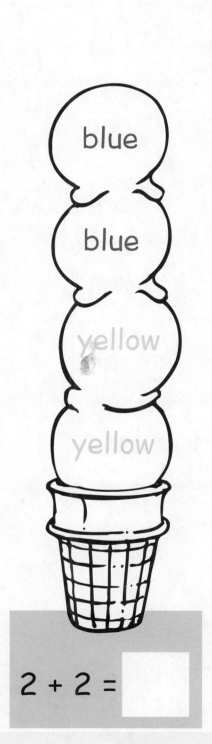
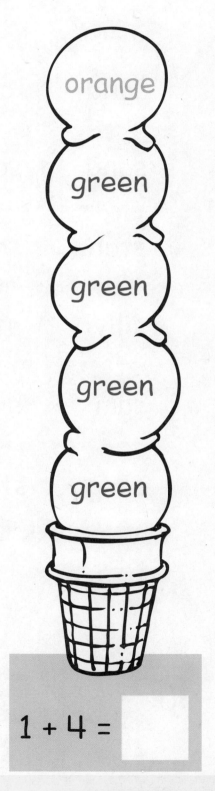

brown
brown
brown
red
red

blue
blue
yellow
yellow

orange
green
green
green
green

3 + 2 =

2 + 2 =

1 + 4 =

Make a Path

Try to get to the beach. Color the word sand.

Start

sand	and	sun	sea	band
sand	sand	dan	some	saw
stand	sand	sand	home	was
silly	star	sand	and	look
sam	song	sand	sand	son
sang	stand	and	sand	sand

Feed the Hungry Elephants

Cut. ✂ Paste the peanuts that rhyme.

ten 10

paste

paste

rose

paste

paste

eight 8

paste

paste

skate

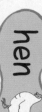

pen

hose

hen

toes

gate

Fast or Slow?

Circle the **fast** ones.

fast

Circle the **slow** one.

slow

78

Count with Me

Color and count.

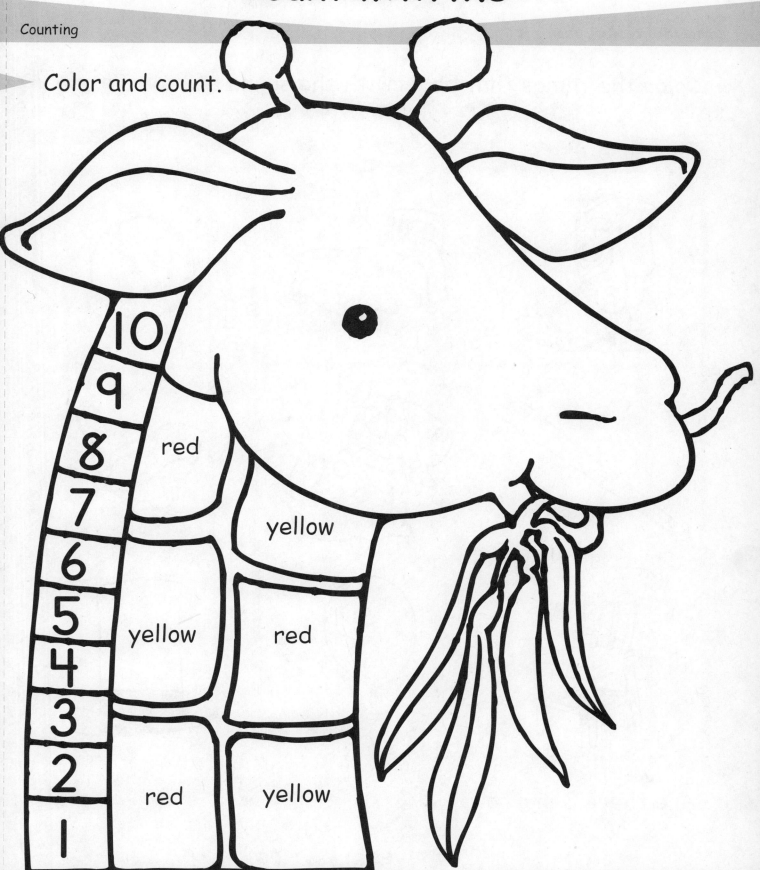

10
9
8 — red
7
6
5 — yellow | red
4
3
2 — red | yellow
1

Listen for the Sound

Letter/Sound Association

Color the things that begin with the sound of b.

 Bb

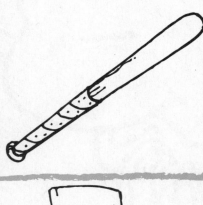  

Are there 3 in a row?

yes   no

Which Bear Lives Where?

Inference

Match the bears to the houses where they live.

Find the Monkey

Color each space the correct color.

82

Oops!

Cut and paste. Put the pictures in order.

1 paste

2 paste

3 paste

Circle the words that are the same.

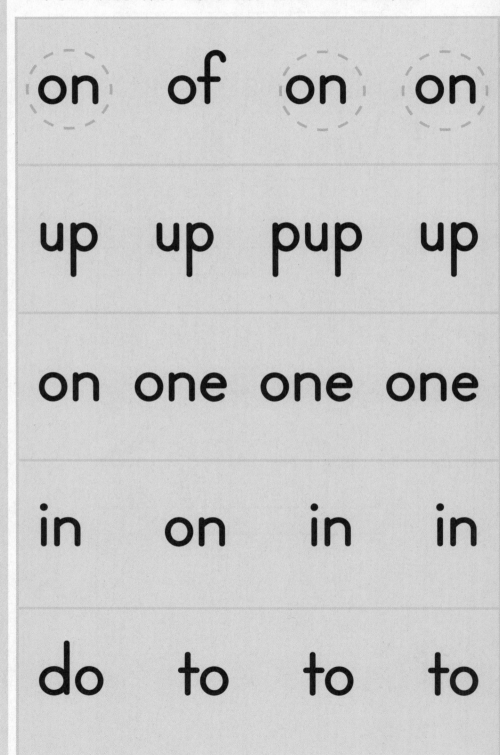

on	of	on	on
up	up	pup	up
on	one	one	one
in	on	in	in
do	to	to	to

Two Blackbirds

Reading Familiar Rhymes

Cut out the two hand puppets. Glue the edges together.
Put your hands inside and say the poem.

Two little blackbirds
Sitting on a hill,
One named Jack,
The other named Jill.
Fly away, Jack.
Fly away, Jill.
Come back, Jack.
Come back, Jill.

fold

Jack

fold

Jill

paste

paste

paste

paste

Yummy!

Count and write.

$3 + 3 = $ ☐

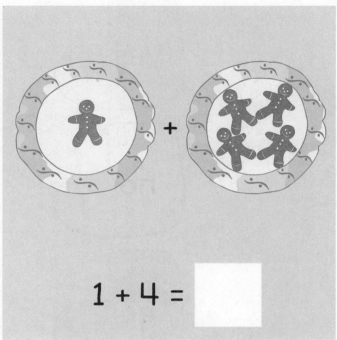

$1 + 4 = $ ☐

$2 + 2 = $ ☐

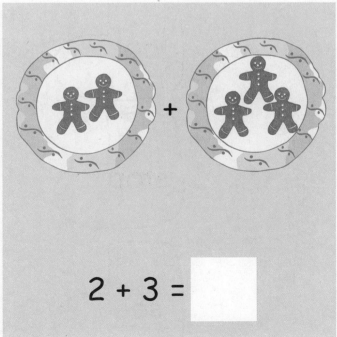

$2 + 3 = $ ☐

Pick the Pairs

Match each pair. Draw a line. Color the sock.

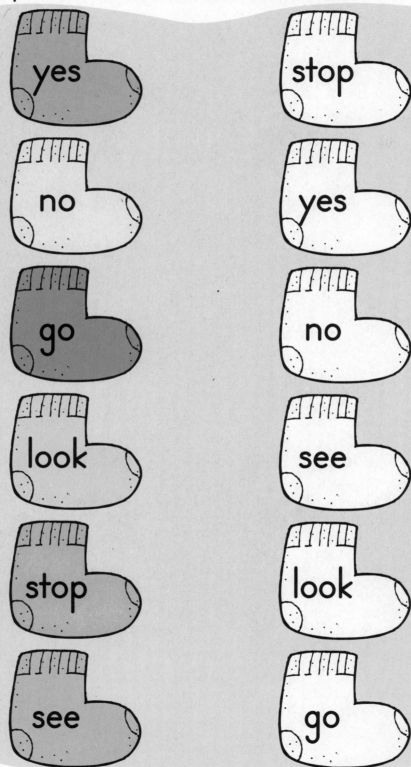

yes

no

go

look

stop

see

stop

yes

no

see

look

go

88

Make It Rhyme

Cut and paste.

bed

queen

paste

bee

tree

paste

bean

jeep

paste

sheep

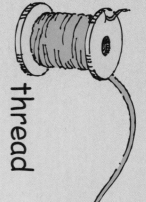

thread

paste

What Is It?

Connect the dots. Count the corners.

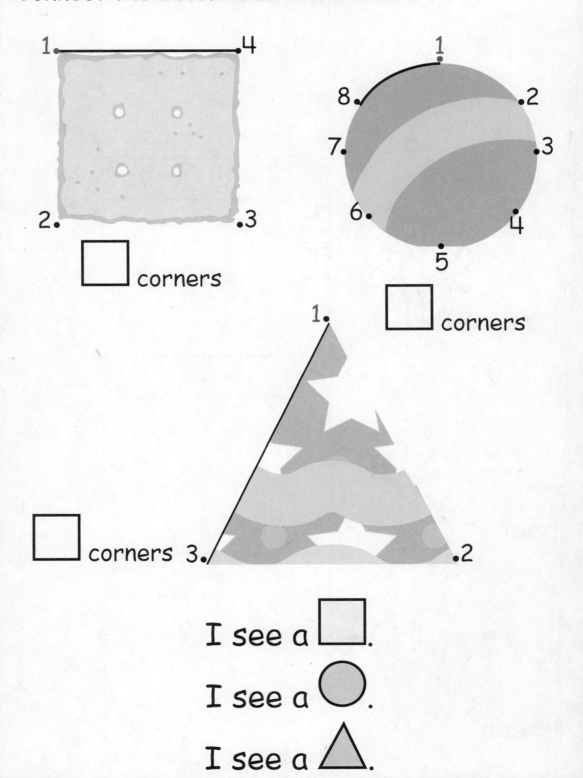

☐ corners

☐ corners

☐ corners

I see a ☐.

I see a ⃝.

I see a △.

Listen for the Sound

Color the things that begin with the sound of w.

Are there 3 in a row?

 yes   no

Dig It Up!

Connect the dots to see what Fido dug up. Start with 1.

What did Fido dig up?

stick   ball   bone

Name the Number

Trace.

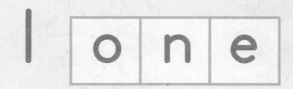

1 o n e

2 t w o

3 t h r e e

Circle.

one two three

one two three

one two three

93

Pretty Patterns

Color the flowers to finish the patterns.

Watch Me Grow

Cut and paste. Put the pictures in order.

1 | paste

2 | paste

3 | paste

Connect the dots. Start with 1.

How old are you? _____

Sleepy Snake

Cut on the – – – line.

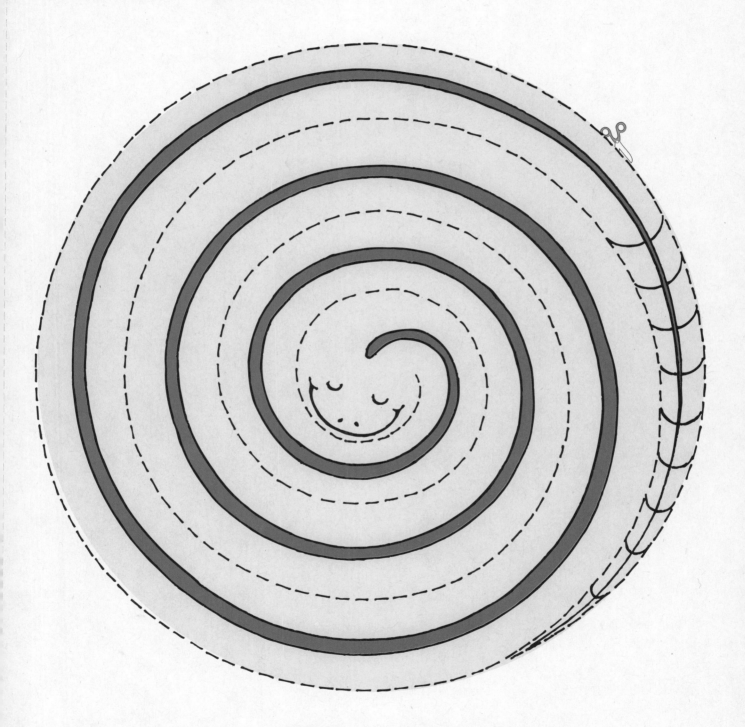

Sleep, snake.

Make a Book

Cut. Put the pages in order. Staple on the side.

MY

NUMBER
BOOK

I can count!

Name _____

staple

staple

EMC 6308 • © Evan-Moor Corp.   The Never-Bored Kid Book 2

one 1

Draw one fish.

EMC 6308 • © Evan-Moor Corp.   The Never-Bored Kid Book 2

three 3

Draw three fish.

EMC 6308 • © Evan-Moor Corp.   The Never-Bored Kid Book 2

five 5

Draw five fish.

EMC 6308 • © Evan-Moor Corp.   The Never-Bored Kid Book 2

2 two

Draw two fish.

1 one
2 two
3 three
4 four
5 five
6 six

6 six

Draw six fish.

4 four

Draw four fish.

Three in a Row

Circle the three letters that are the same. Draw a line through them.

m	n	w
w	m	u
n	u	m

p	d	b
p	q	d
p	b	q

r	f	t
j	f	k
l	f	j

e	g	h
c	c	c
o	e	g

What Is Missing?

Draw what is missing. Color the snails.

Hungry Kitty

Color the kitty.

kitty

orange

Kitty had a snack. How many are left?

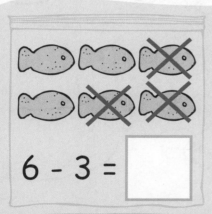

6 - 3 = ☐

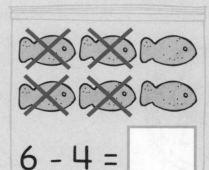

6 - 4 = ☐

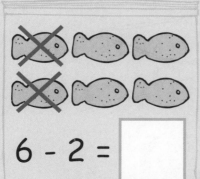

6 - 2 = ☐

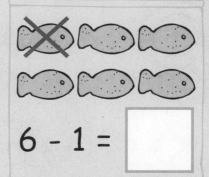

6 - 1 = ☐

Color a Rhyme

Color the two things in each row that rhyme.

Stop and Go

Cut. Put the pages in order. Staple on the side.

staple

staple

Stop and Go

Name _____

EMC 6308 • © Evan-Moor Corp.   The Never-Bored Kid Book 2

1

Stop!

EMC 6308 • © Evan-Moor Corp.   The Never-Bored Kid Book 2

3

Stop!

EMC 6308 • © Evan-Moor Corp.   The Never-Bored Kid Book 2

5

Stop!

EMC 6308 • © Evan-Moor Corp.   The Never-Bored Kid Book 2

2

Go.

Stop!

Wait!

Go!

6

Go, go, go!

4

Go.

Rick Robot

Color the s.

How many did you find?

five   six   eight

Listen for the Sound

Letter/Sound Association

Color the things that begin with the sound of **h**.

Are there 3 in a row?

yes

no

Two Towers

Cut and paste. Make a tower to match.

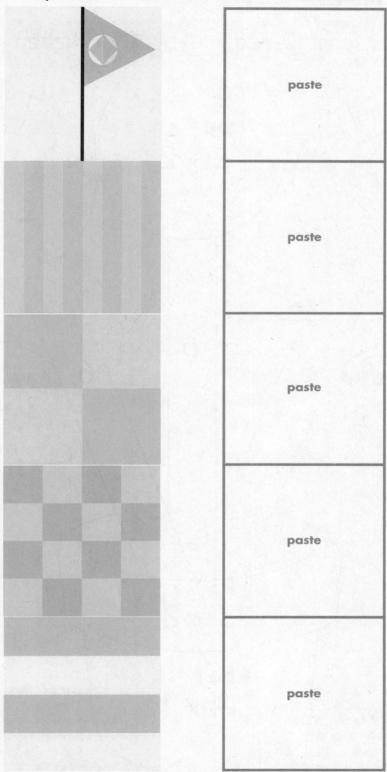

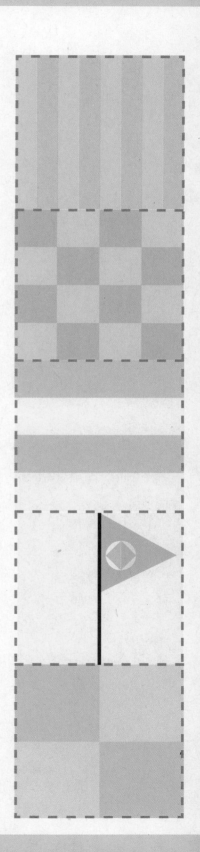

The Tulips

Count and color.

3-yellow   5-red   4-blue   6-green

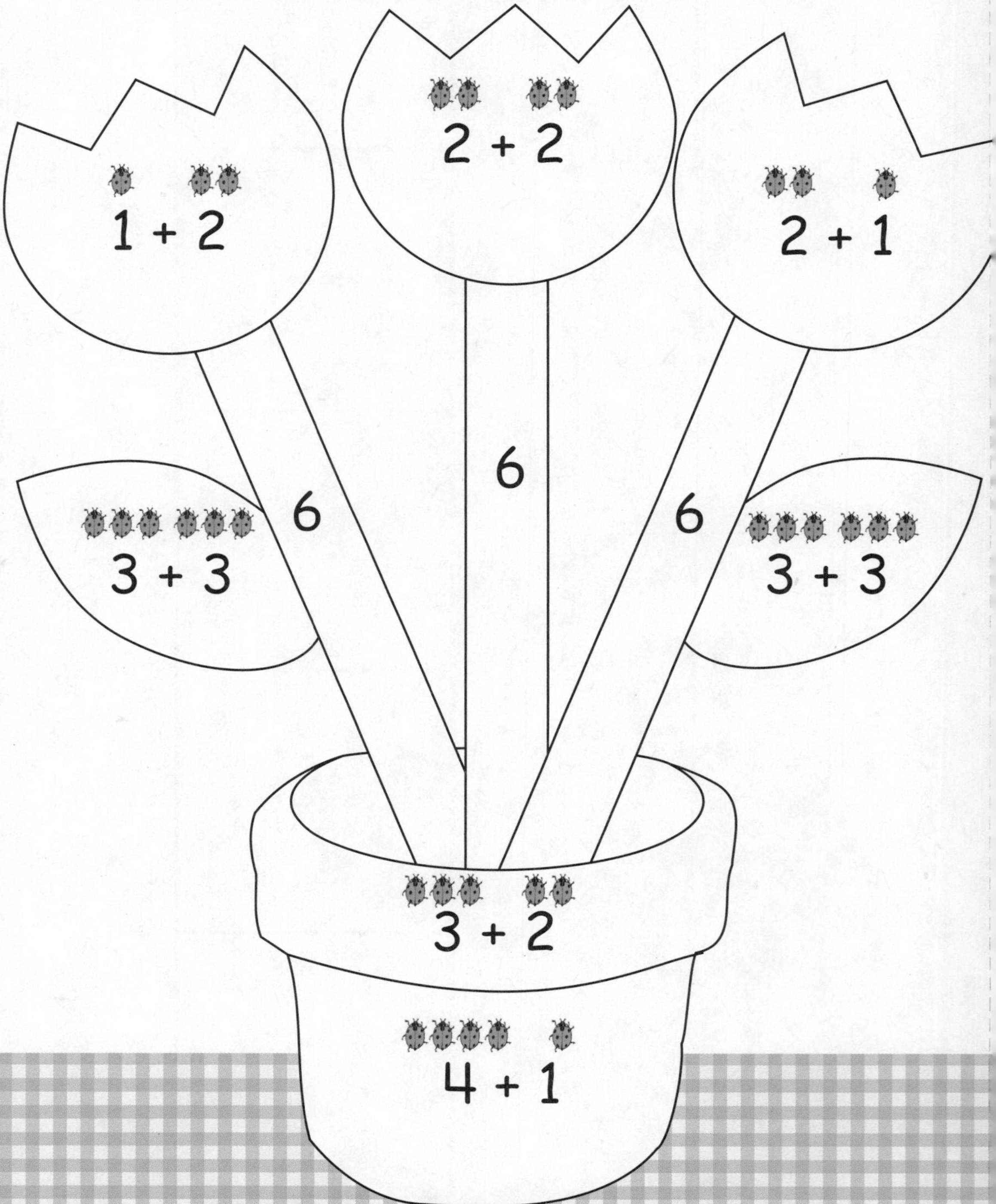

2 + 2

1 + 2

2 + 1

6

6

6

3 + 3

3 + 3

3 + 2

4 + 1

Letter Patterns

Write the letters to finish the patterns.

b a a b a a _____

m o o m o o _____

m e o w m e o w _____

a r f a r f _____

Out in Space

Follow the stars to the moon.

1

2

3

4

5

6

7   8

9

10

11

12

13

14

15

16

17

18

19

20

Hey, diddle, diddle.
The cat and the fiddle,
The cow jumped over the moon.

Pretty Blocks

Copy the pattern.

113

Off to the Races

Draw a race car.

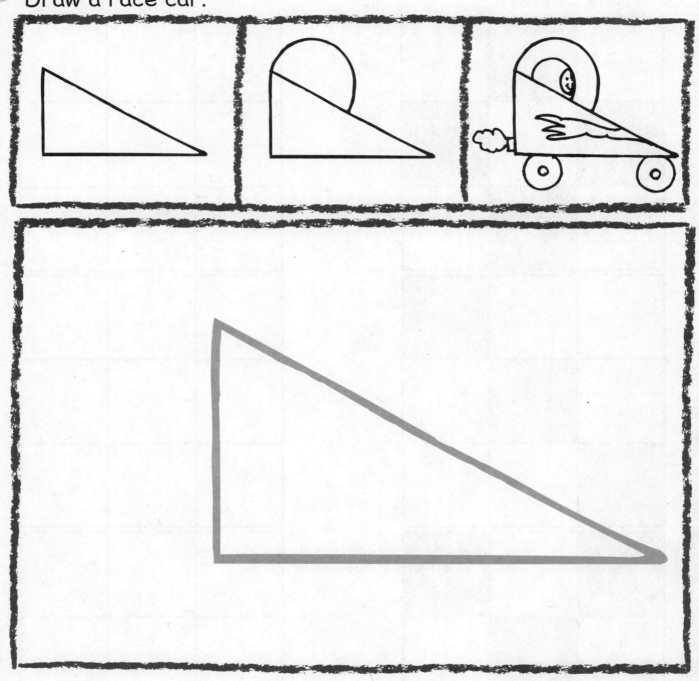

Will you win the race?

 yes

 no

114

Three Hungry Kittens

Three hungry little kittens cried,
"Mamma dear,
May we please have some pie?"

Color 3.

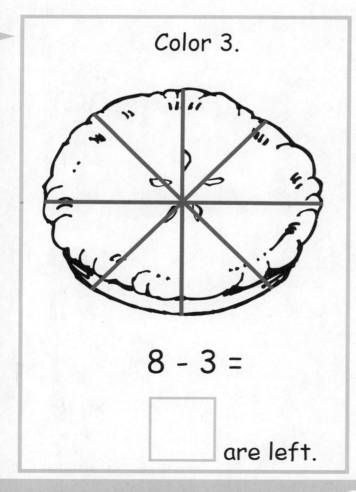

8 - 3 =

☐ are left.

Color 3.

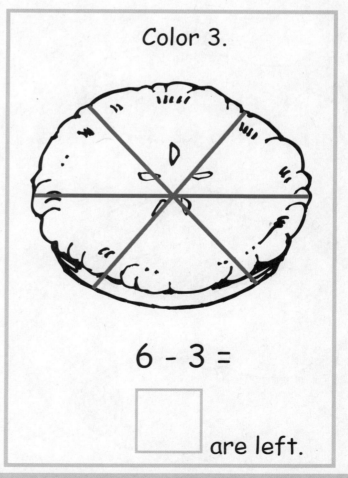

6 - 3 =

☐ are left.

Five Little Fish

Find the rhyme and trace the way home for each fish.

Make a Book

Color. Cut. Put the pages in order. Staple on the side.

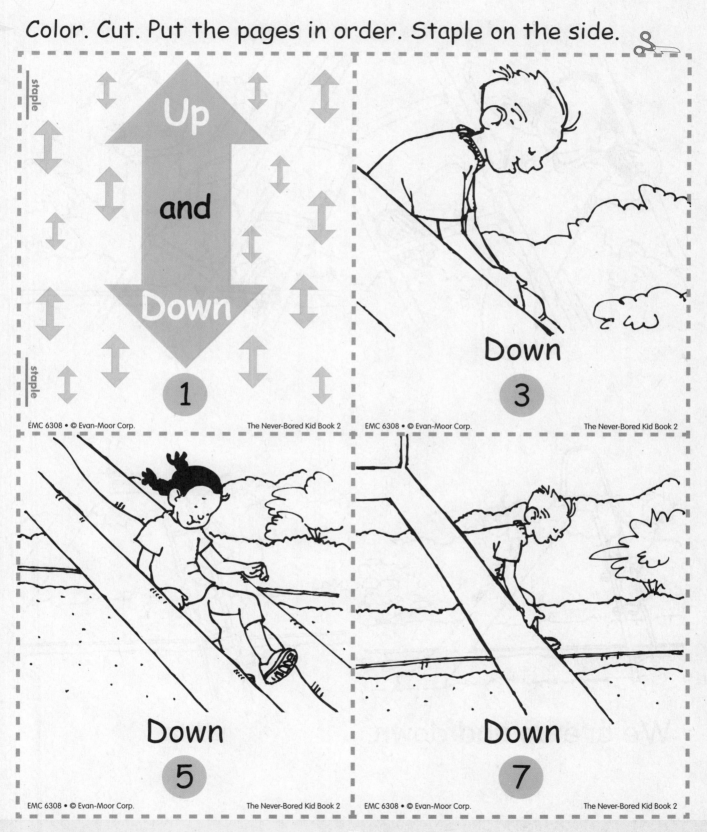

staple

Up and Down

1

EMC 6308 • © Evan-Moor Corp.   The Never-Bored Kid Book 2

Down

3

EMC 6308 • © Evan-Moor Corp.   The Never-Bored Kid Book 2

Down

5

EMC 6308 • © Evan-Moor Corp.   The Never-Bored Kid Book 2

Down

7

EMC 6308 • © Evan-Moor Corp.   The Never-Bored Kid Book 2

Up

4

Up

2

We are up **and** down.

8

Up

6

What's Wrong?

Circle the things that are wrong.

Listen for the Sound

Color the things that begin with the sound of p.

Pp

Are there 3 in a row?

yes

no

See Spot

Color the picture.

can

up.

Spot

sit

Cut and paste. Put the words in order.

paste	paste	paste	paste

Stripes and Dots

Color to finish the patterns.

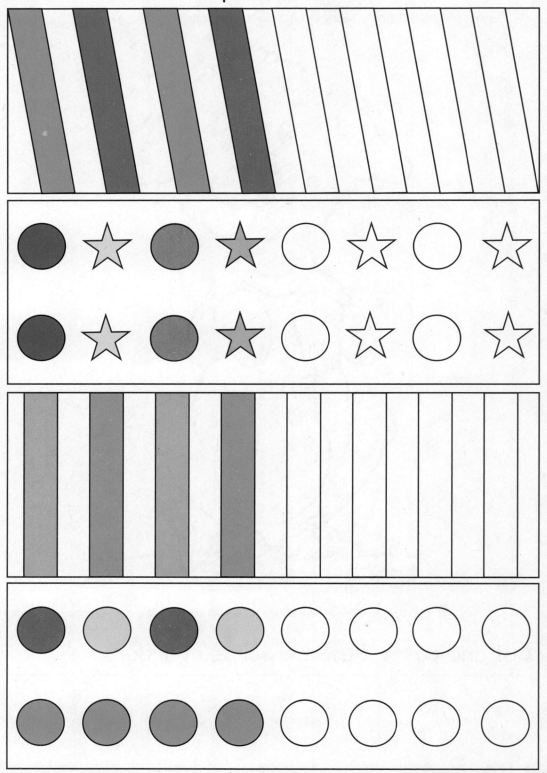

122

Run, Rabbit, Run

Help Rabbit win the race.
Follow the word **run** to the finish line.

run	run	sun	nut	go	me
no	run	run	fast	in	see
fun	nest	run	to	up	yes
blue	up	run	run	run	nine
box	six	by	on	run	run

FINISH

My Marbles

Write the numbers to tell how many.

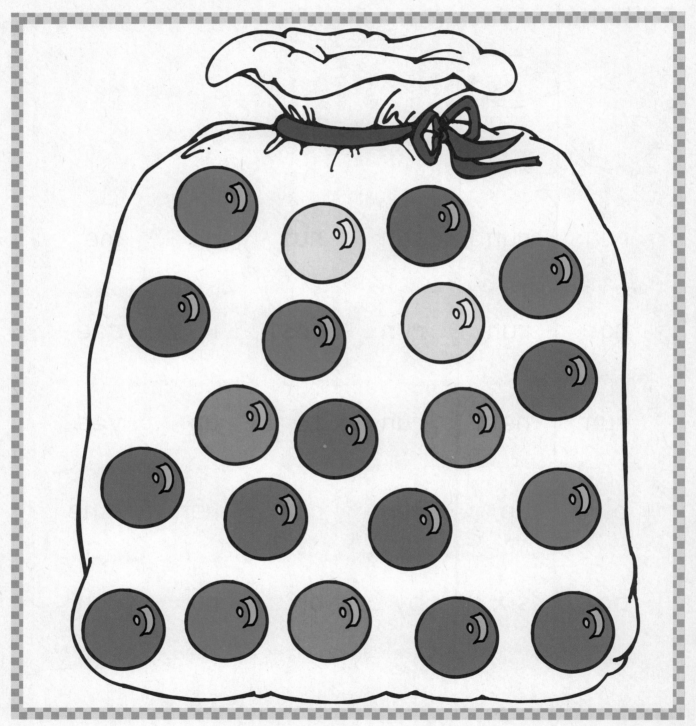

red _____   yellow _____   blue _____   green _____

Read and Draw

Finish the pictures.

two red

three blue

one green

two purple

Happy Hippo

Finish the hippo. Color it.

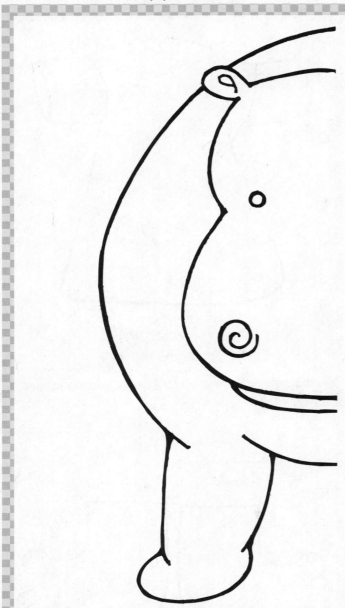

Circle what makes Hippo happy.

Listen for the Sound

Color the things that begin with the sound of n.

Nn

Are there 3 in a row?

yes

no

What's Inside?

Connect the dots to find out what is in the cave.
Start with 1.

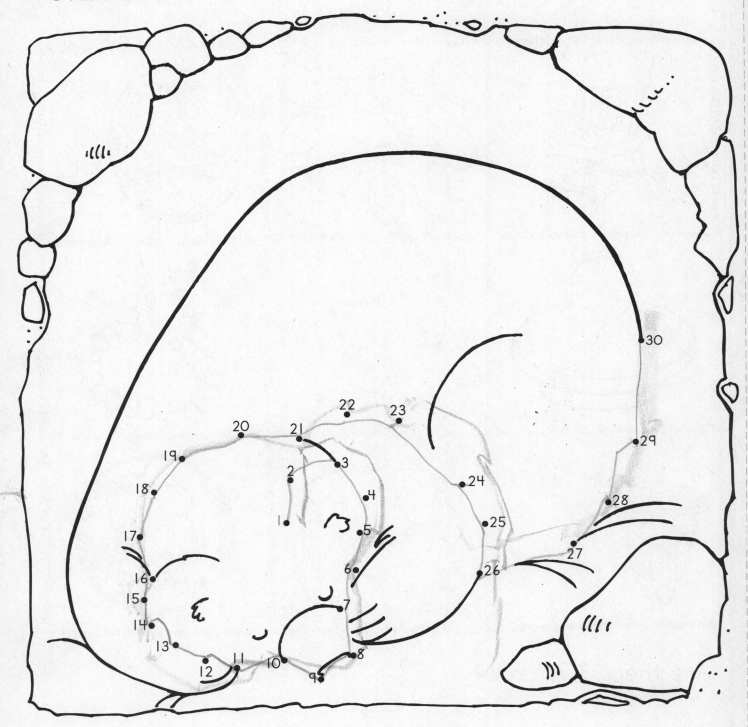

Animal Farm

Draw to match.

mouse

chick

puppy

I did it all!

Give me a star!

_____

Name

Glue

My Color Chart

red

yellow

orange

blue

green

purple

brown

black

white

Answer Key

Checking your child's work is an important part of learning. It allows you to see what your child knows well and what areas need more practice. It also provides an opportunity for you to help your child understand that making mistakes is a part of learning.

When an error is discovered, ask your child to look carefully at the question or problem. Errors often occur through misreading. Your child can quickly correct these errors. Help your child with items she or he finds difficult.

Page 4

Page 5

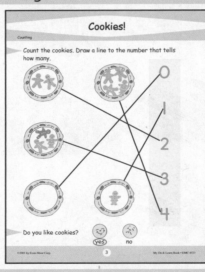

Page 6

Page 7

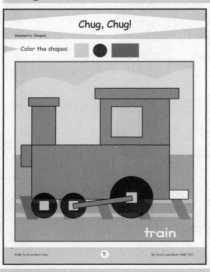

Page 8

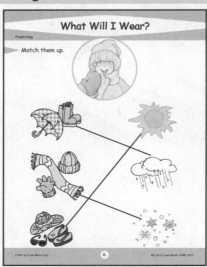

Page 9

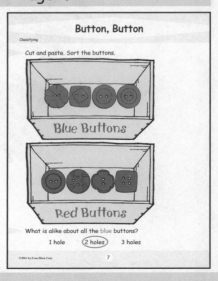

Page 10

Where Is Alf's Bone?

Tracking

Help Alf find his bone.

8

My Do & Learn Book • EMC 4523

Page 11

Happy Octopus

Counting

Trace the numbers.

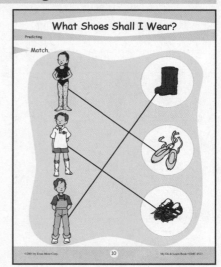

Count.

1 2 3 4 5 6 7 8

My octopus has **8** arms.

9

My Do & Learn Book • EMC 4523

Page 12

What Shoes Shall I Wear?

Predicting

Match.

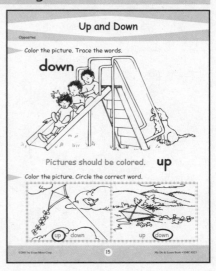

10

My Do & Learn Book • EMC 4523

Page 15

Name That Color!

Reading Color Words

Fill in the boxes.

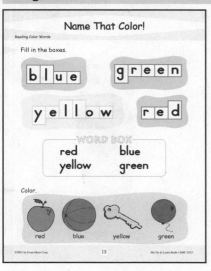

blue   green

yellow   red

WORD BOX
red   blue
yellow   green

Color.

red   blue   yellow   green

13

My Do & Learn Book • EMC 4523

Page 16

Tweet Tweet

Visual Discrimination

Color each part.

h=blue   n=brown   u=yellow

How many birds?   one   (two)

14

My Do & Learn Book • EMC 4523

Page 17

Up and Down

Opposites

Color the picture. Trace the words.

down

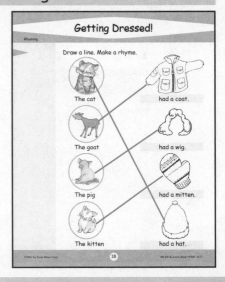

Pictures should be colored.   **up**

Color the picture. Circle the correct word.

(up) down   up (down)

15

My Do & Learn Book • EMC 4523

Page 18

Five Red Apples

Subtraction

Read and count.

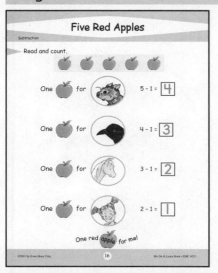

One 🍎 for 🐱   5 - 1 = 4

One 🍎 for 🐦   4 - 1 = 3

One 🍎 for 🐴   3 - 1 = 2

One 🍎 for 🐶   2 - 1 = 1

One red 🍎 for me!

16

My Do & Learn Book • EMC 4523

Page 19

Fish Spots

Counting

Cut and paste the fish.
Count the dots on each fish.

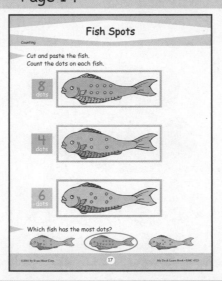

8 dots

4 dots

6 dots

Which fish has the most dots?

17

My Do & Learn Book • EMC 4523

Page 20

Getting Dressed!

Rhyming

Draw a line. Make a rhyme.

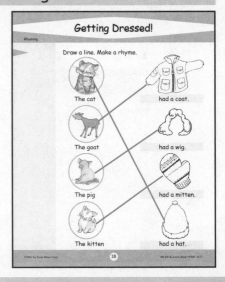

The cat   had a coat.

The goat   had a wig.

The pig   had a mitten.

The kitten   had a hat.

18

My Do & Learn Book • EMC 4523

Page 21

Listen for the Sound

Letter/Sound Association

Color the things that begin with the sound of l.

Ll

Are there 3 in a row? yes   no

©2001 by Evan-Moor Corp.   19   My Do & Learn Book • EMC 4523

Page 22

How Would You Feel?

Inference

Circle happy or sad.

happy / sad
happy / sad
happy / sad
happy / sad
happy / sad
happy / sad

©2001 by Evan-Moor Corp.   20   My Do & Learn Book • EMC 4523

Page 23

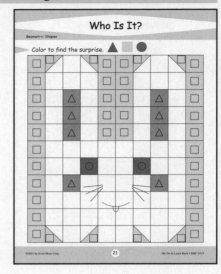

Who Is It?

Geometric Shapes

Color to find the surprise. ▲ ■ ●

©2001 by Evan-Moor Corp.   21   My Do & Learn Book • EMC 4523

Page 24

What Will Happen?

Predicting

Draw a line. Show what will happen.

©2001 by Evan-Moor Corp.   22   My Do & Learn Book • EMC 4523

Page 25

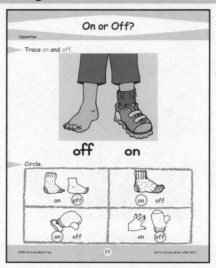

On or Off?

Opposites

Trace on and off.

off   **on**

Circle.

on / off   on / off
on / off   on / off

©2001 by Evan-Moor Corp.   23   My Do & Learn Book • EMC 4523

Page 26

Ice Cream

Visual Discrimination

Color to match.

Trace.

ice cream

©2001 by Evan-Moor Corp.   24   My Do & Learn Book • EMC 4523

Page 27

Little Bo Peep

Tracking

Help her find her pet.

©2001 by Evan-Moor Corp.   25   My Do & Learn Book • EMC 4523

Page 28

Turtle

Counting

Connect the dots. Start with 1.

Count the turtles.

1 2 3 4 5 6 7 8 9 10

©2001 by Evan-Moor Corp.   26   My Do & Learn Book • EMC 4523

Page 29

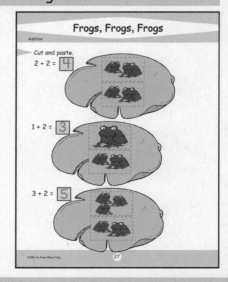

Frogs, Frogs, Frogs

Addition

Cut and paste.

$2 + 2 = 4$

$1 + 2 = 3$

$3 + 2 = 5$

©2001 by Evan-Moor Corp.   27   My Do & Learn Book • EMC 4523

Cheese Treats
Tracking

Trace 3 paths from 🐭 to 🧀.

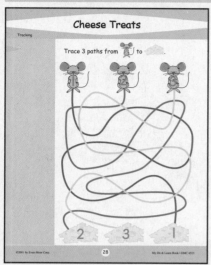

©2001 by Evan-Moor Corp. · 28 · My Do & Learn Book • EMC 4523

Find Red
Visual Discrimination

Trace and color.

red

Find red and circle.

m	r e d
r e d	m
m	r e d
r e d	m

How many red? 4

©2001 by Evan-Moor Corp. · 29 · My Do & Learn Book • EMC 4523

Blast Off!
Following Directions, Counting

Draw a rocket. Count down to blast off.

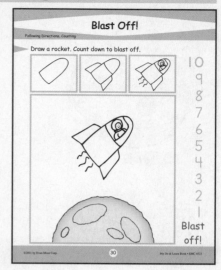

10 9 8 7 6 5 4 3 2 1

Blast off!

©2001 by Evan-Moor Corp. · 30 · My Do & Learn Book • EMC 4523

Listen for the Sound
Letter/Sound Association

Color the things that begin with the sound of f.

Ff

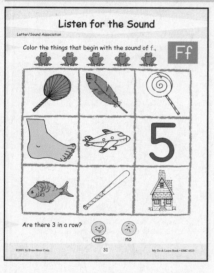

Are there 3 in a row? yes no

©2001 by Evan-Moor Corp. · 31 · My Do & Learn Book • EMC 4523

What Will It Be?
Inference

Draw a picture to show what it will be.

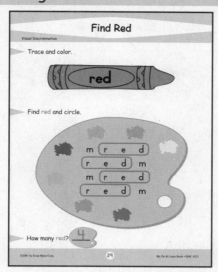

Picture of a stack of pancakes.

Picture of a bowl of salad.

Picture of a flower.

©2001 by Evan-Moor Corp. · 32 · My Do & Learn Book • EMC 4523

Color Fun
Reading Color Words

Write the words.

green **purple**

yellow

WORD BOX
purple   green   yellow

Color it.

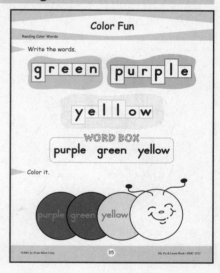

purple green yellow

©2001 by Evan-Moor Corp. · 35 · My Do & Learn Book • EMC 4523

Going Camping
Classifying

Circle what you would take on a camping trip.

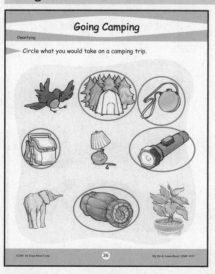

©2001 by Evan-Moor Corp. · 36 · My Do & Learn Book • EMC 4523

9, 10, A Big Fat ____
Counting

Draw lines to connect the dots. Start with 1.

Trace.

1 2 3 4 5
6 7 8 9 10

©2001 by Evan-Moor Corp. · 37 · My Do & Learn Book • EMC 4523

I Can Rhyme
Rhyming Words

Draw a line from the word to the picture.

man
can
fan

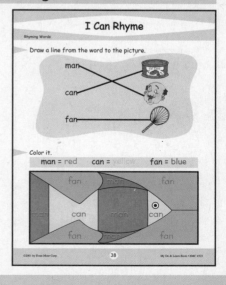

Color it.

man = red   can = yellow   fan = blue

©2001 by Evan-Moor Corp. · 38 · My Do & Learn Book • EMC 4523

Page 41

Fill It!

Visual Discrimination

Cut. Paste.

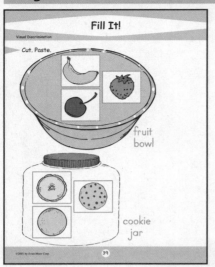

fruit bowl

cookie jar

©2001 by Evan-Moor Corp. 39 My Do & Learn Book • EMC 4523

Page 42

Which Is Heavier?

Comparisons

Circle the one that is heavier.

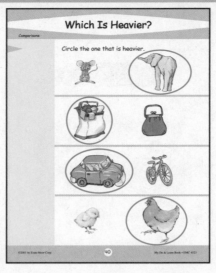

©2001 by Evan-Moor Corp. 40 My Do & Learn Book • EMC 4523

Page 43

Jack and Jill

Tracking

Trace a path for Jack. Trace a path for Jill.

Jack and Jill
Went up the hill
To fetch a pail of water.
Jack fell down
And broke his crown
And Jill came tumbling after.

©2001 by Evan-Moor Corp. 41 My Do & Learn Book • EMC 4523

Page 44

Have a Slice

Counting

Connect the dots. Start with 1.

How many seeds in this slice? 9

©2001 by Evan-Moor Corp. 42 My Do & Learn Book • EMC 4523

Page 45

Colorful Squares!

Visual Discrimination

Match the parts that make a square.

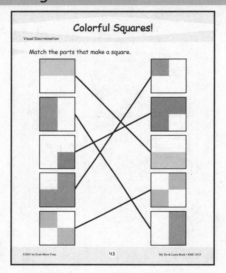

©2001 by Evan-Moor Corp. 43 My Do & Learn Book • EMC 4523

Page 46

Little Ducky Duddle

Following Directions

Draw Ducky Duddle.

Little Ducky Duddle went wading in a puddle.

©2001 by Evan-Moor Corp. 44 My Do & Learn Book • EMC 4523

Page 47

I Can Count

Counting

Trace the numbers.

10 9 8 7 6 5 4 3 2 1

Count backward from 10 to 1. Color the boxes.

©2001 by Evan-Moor Corp. 45 My Do & Learn Book • EMC 4523

Page 48

Piggy Bank

Counting

Connect the dots. Start with 1. Count the pennies.

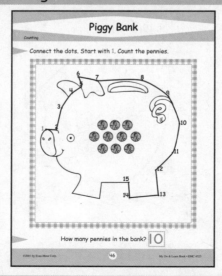

How many pennies in the bank? 10

©2001 by Evan-Moor Corp. 46 My Do & Learn Book • EMC 4523

Page 51

Listen for the Sound

Letter/Sound Association

Color the things that begin with the sound of d.

Dd

Are there 3 in a row?   yes   no

©2001 by Evan-Moor Corp. 49 My Do & Learn Book • EMC 4523

Where Is Maddy Going?
Inference

Maddy has a 🧳

Maddy has a ✏️

Maddy has a 📓

Maddy has a 🎒

Maddy is going to the __school__

school   park   beach

©2001 by Evan-Moor Corp.   50   My Do & Learn Book • EMC 4523

Elmer Elephant
Geometric Shapes

Color the shapes.

Circle what Elmer would like to eat.

©2001 by Evan-Moor Corp.   51   My Do & Learn Book • EMC 4523

Wiggle Worm
Patterning

Continue the pattern.

©2001 by Evan-Moor Corp.   52   My Do & Learn Book • EMC 4523

Helicopter Tricks
Tracking

Help the helicopter land.

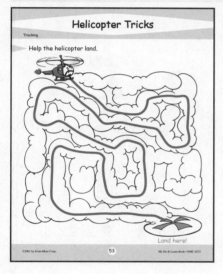

Land here!

©2001 by Evan-Moor Corp.   53   My Do & Learn Book • EMC 4523

Timothy Turtle
Visual Discrimination

Color to match.

Timothy Turtle likes you!

©2001 by Evan-Moor Corp.   54   My Do & Learn Book • EMC 4523

Bugs Galore!
Addition

Solve the problems.

$2 + 2 = 4$ $4 + 2 = 6$

$3 + 3 = 6$ $2 + 3 = 5$

$4 + 0 = 4$ $1 + 3 = 4$

©2001 by Evan-Moor Corp.   55   My Do & Learn Book • EMC 4523

Just the Same
Visual Discrimination

Match the shapes.

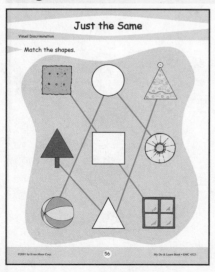

©2001 by Evan-Moor Corp.   56   My Do & Learn Book • EMC 4523

Clancy the Clown
Following Directions

Draw Clancy.

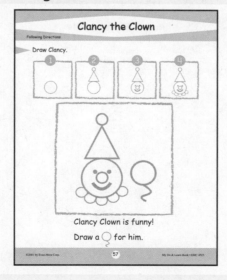

Clancy Clown is funny!
Draw a ◯ for him.

©2001 by Evan-Moor Corp.   57   My Do & Learn Book • EMC 4523

Good Morning!
Counting

Connect the dots. Start with 1.

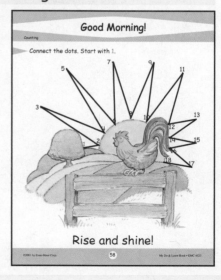

Rise and shine!

©2001 by Evan-Moor Corp.   58   My Do & Learn Book • EMC 4523

Find the Rhyme

Rhyming

Cut and paste.

fan — man
hat — bat
dog — frog
skate — gate

59

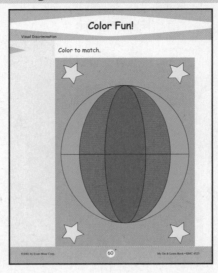

Color Fun!

Visual Discrimination

Color to match.

60

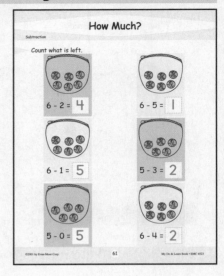

How Much?

Subtraction

Count what is left.

6 - 2 = 4   6 - 5 = 1
6 - 1 = 5   5 - 3 = 2
5 - 0 = 5   6 - 4 = 2

61

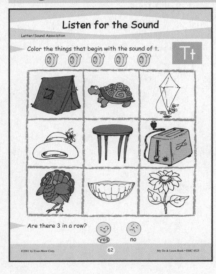

Listen for the Sound

Letter/Sound Association

Color the things that begin with the sound of t.

Tt

Are there 3 in a row?   yes   no

62

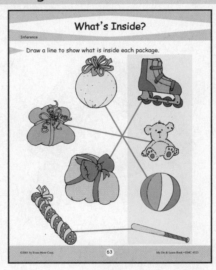

What's Inside?

Inference

Draw a line to show what is inside each package.

63

A Shape Picture

Geometric Shapes

Color the shapes.

Count the shapes.

● 5   ▲ 2   ■ 2   ▬ 3

64

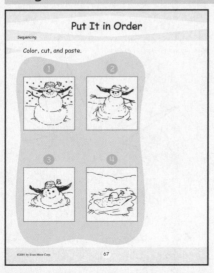

Put It in Order

Sequencing

Color, cut, and paste.

① ②
③ ④

67

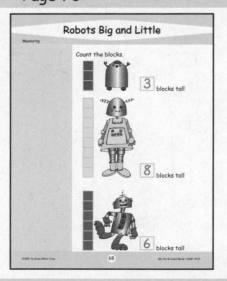

Robots Big and Little

Measuring

Count the blocks.

3 blocks tall
8 blocks tall
6 blocks tall

68

Rock-a-Bye Baby

Predicting

Color what Baby needs.

69

Flying High

Where Will You See Me?
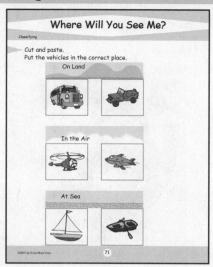

Let's Take a Ride

Count the Scoops

Make a Path
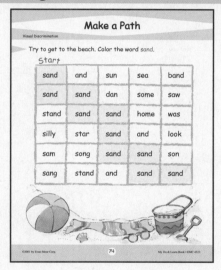

Feed the Hungry Elephants

Fast or Slow?

Count with Me

Listen for the Sound

Page 81

Which Bear Lives Where?

Inference

Match the bears to the houses where they live.

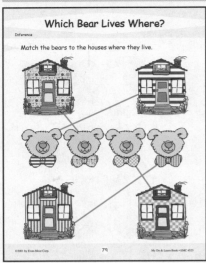

©2001 by Evan-Moor Corp.   79   My Do & Learn Book • EMC 4523

Page 82

Find the Monkey

Geometric Shapes

Color each space the correct color.

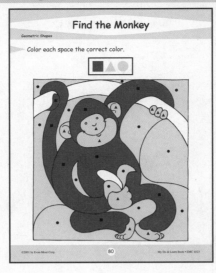

©2001 by Evan-Moor Corp.   80   My Do & Learn Book • EMC 4523

Page 83

Oops!

Visual Discrimination

Cut and paste. Put the pictures in order.

©2001 by Evan-Moor Corp.   81   My Do & Learn Book • EMC 4523

Page 84

Look Carefully

Visual Discrimination

Circle the words that are the same.

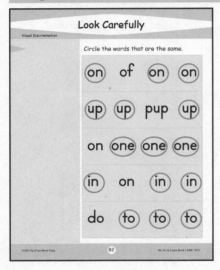

©2001 by Evan-Moor Corp.   82   My Do & Learn Book • EMC 4523

Page 87

Yummy!

Addition

Count and write.

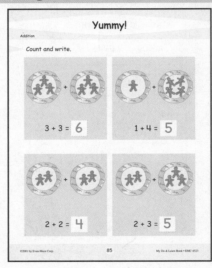

$3 + 3 = 6$ $1 + 4 = 5$

$2 + 2 = 4$ $2 + 3 = 5$

©2001 by Evan-Moor Corp.   85   My Do & Learn Book • EMC 4523

Page 88

Pick the Pairs

Visual Discrimination

Match each pair. Draw a line. Color the sock.

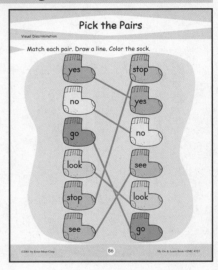

©2001 by Evan-Moor Corp.   86   My Do & Learn Book • EMC 4523

Page 89

Make It Rhyme

Rhyming

Cut and paste.

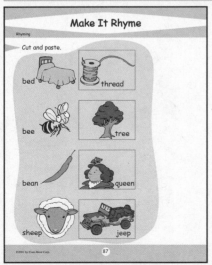

©2001 by Evan-Moor Corp.   87   My Do & Learn Book • EMC 4523

Page 90

What Is It?

Geometric Shapes

Connect the dots. Count the corners.

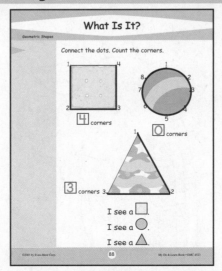

4 corners

0 corners

3 corners

I see a ☐.
I see a ◯.
I see a △.

©2001 by Evan-Moor Corp.   88   My Do & Learn Book • EMC 4523

Page 91

Listen for the Sound

Letter/Sound Association

Color the things that begin with the sound of w.

Are there 3 in a row?   yes   no

©2001 by Evan-Moor Corp.   89   My Do & Learn Book • EMC 4523

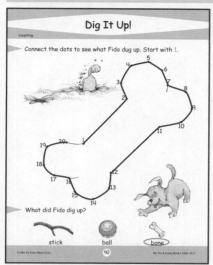

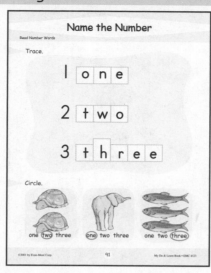

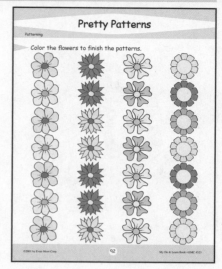

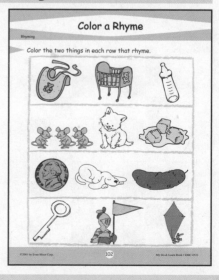

Page 107

Rick Robot

Visual Discrimination

Color the s.

How many did you find?

five   six   (eight)

©2001 by Evan-Moor Corp.   105   My Do & Learn Book • EMC 4523

Page 108

Listen for the Sound

Letter/Sound Association

Color the things that begin with the sound of h.   Hh

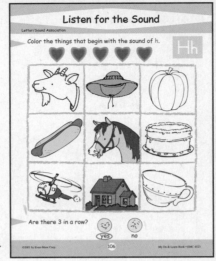

Are there 3 in a row?   (yes)   no

©2001 by Evan-Moor Corp.   106   My Do & Learn Book • EMC 4523

Page 109

Two Towers

Sequencing

Cut and paste. Make a tower to match.

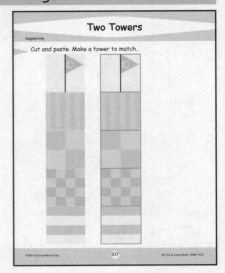

©2001 by Evan-Moor Corp.   107   My Do & Learn Book • EMC 4523

Page 110

The Tulips

Addition

Count and color.

3-   5-red   4-blue   6-green

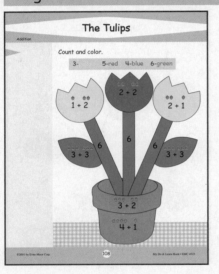

©2001 by Evan-Moor Corp.   108   My Do & Learn Book • EMC 4523

Page 111

Letter Patterns

Patterning

Write the letters to finish the patterns.

baabaa **b a a b a a**

moomoo **m o o m o o**

meowmeow **m e o w**

arfarf **a r f a r f**

©2001 by Evan-Moor Corp.   109   My Do & Learn Book • EMC 4523

Page 112

Out in Space

Number Order

Follow the stars to the moon.

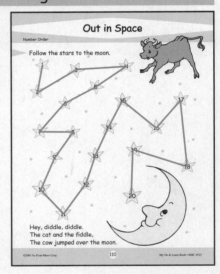

Hey, diddle, diddle.
The cat and the fiddle,
The cow jumped over the moon.

©2001 by Evan-Moor Corp.   110   My Do & Learn Book • EMC 4523

Page 113

Pretty Blocks

Visual Discrimination

Copy the pattern.

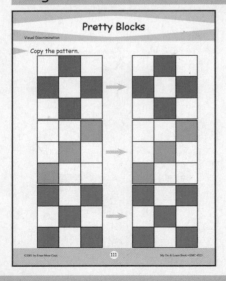

©2001 by Evan-Moor Corp.   111   My Do & Learn Book • EMC 4523

Page 114

Off to the Races

Following Directions

Draw a race car.

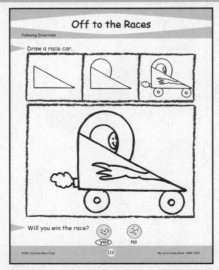

Will you win the race?   (yes)   no

©2001 by Evan-Moor Corp.   112   My Do & Learn Book • EMC 4523

Page 115

Three Hungry Kittens

Subtraction

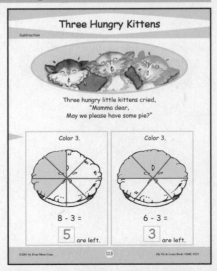

Three hungry little kittens cried,
"Mamma dear,
May we please have some pie?"

Color 3.   Color 3.

$8 - 3 =$ $6 - 3 =$

5 are left.   3 are left.

©2001 by Evan-Moor Corp.   113   My Do & Learn Book • EMC 4523

Page 116

Five Little Fish
Rhyming

Find the rhyme and trace the way home for each fish.

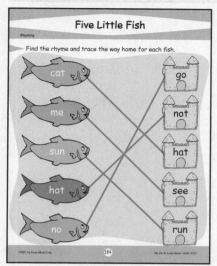

cat — hat
me — see
sun — run
hot — not
no — go

Page 119

What's Wrong?
Visual Discrimination

Circle the things that are wrong.

Page 120

Listen for the Sound
Letter/Sound Association

Color the things that begin with the sound of p.

Pp

Are there 3 in a row?   yes   no

Page 121

See Spot
Sequencing

Color the picture.

Picture should be colored.

Cut and paste. Put the words in order.

| Spot | can | sit | up. |

Page 122

Stripes and Dots
Patterning

Color to finish the patterns.

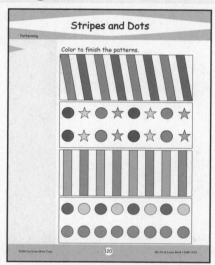

Page 123

Run, Rabbit, Run
Visual Discrimination

Help Rabbit win the race.
Follow the word run to the finish line.

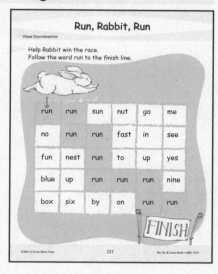

run	run	sun	nut	go	me
no	run	run	fast	in	see
fun	nest	run	to	up	yes
blue	up	run	run	run	nine
box	six	by	on	run	run

FINISH

Page 124

My Marbles
Counting

Write the numbers to tell how many.

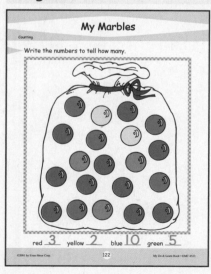

red 3   yellow 2   blue 10   green 5

Page 125

Read and Draw
Reading Sight Words

Finish the pictures.

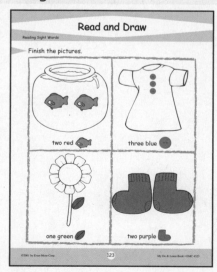

two red
three blue
one green
two purple

Page 126

Happy Hippo
Following Directions

Finish the hippo. Color it.

Circle what makes Hippo happy. Answers will vary.

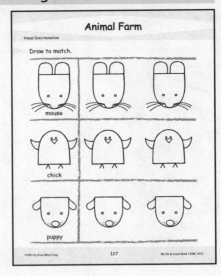